Six Key Communication Skills for Records and Information Managers

CHANDOS
INFORMATION PROFESSIONAL SERIES

Series Editor: Ruth Rikowski
(email: *Rikowskigr@aol.com*)

Chandos' new series of books is aimed at the busy information professional. They have been specially commissioned to provide the reader with an authoritative view of current thinking. They are designed to provide easy-to-read and (most importantly) practical coverage of topics that are of interest to librarians and other information professionals. If you would like a full listing of current and forthcoming titles, please visit our website, *www.chandospublishing.com*

New authors: we are always pleased to receive ideas for new titles; if you would like to write a book for Chandos, please contact Dr Glyn Jones on *g.jones.2@elsevier.com* or telephone +44(0) 1865 843000.

Six Key
Communication Skills
for Records and Information
Managers

KENNETH LAURENCE NEAL

ELSEVIER

AMSTERDAM · BOSTON · CAMBRIDGE · HEIDELBERG · LONDON
NEW YORK · OXFORD · PARIS · SAN DIEGO
SAN FRANCISCO · SINGAPORE · SYDNEY · TOKYO
Chandos Publishing is an imprint of Elsevier

CHANDOS
PUBLISHING

Chandos Publishing
Elsevier Limited
The Boulevard
Langford Lane
Kidlington
Oxford OX5 1GB
UK
store.elsevier.com/Chandos-Publishing-/IMP_207/

Chandos Publishing is an imprint of Elsevier Limited

Tel: +44 (0) 1865 843000
Fax: +44 (0) 1865 843010
store.elsevier.com

First published in 2014

ISBN: 978-1-84334-782-8 (print)
ISBN: 978-1-78063-463-0 (online)

Library of Congress Control Number: 2014938139

British Library Cataloguing-in-Publication Data.
A catalogue record for this book is available from the British Library.

Project management by Neil Shuttlewood Associates, Gt Yarmouth, Norfolk, UK

For my wife, Joann Milano Neal who has given me so much encouragement and support throughout my career

Contents

List of tables

List of abbreviations

AIIM	Association for Information and Image Management
ARMA	Association of Records Managers and Administrators
BPO	Business Process Outsourcing
ECM	Electronic Content Management
GAAP	Generally Accepted Accounting Principles
GUI	Graphical User Interface
HR	Human Resources
ISDN	Integrated Services Digital Network
ISP	Internet Service Provider
IT	Information Technology
ROI	Return On Investment
VDN	Vector Directory Number

Acknowledgements

This book would not have been possible without the support of business colleagues, records managers and information technology professionals. They provided insights, stories and suggestions that helped spotlight why effective communication is so important not only in business, but in our everyday lives.

I would also like to thank the team at Chandos Publishing for their collaboration and support and for giving me the opportunity to communicate a message that I am passionate about.

Finally, in addition to my wife to whom this book is dedicated, I would like to thank my family. My brothers, Marc and David, have always been and always will be more than brothers to me; they have been my friends. And to my parents I owe a lifelong love of the written and spoken word. From the time they helped me craft my first speech about the Statue of Liberty, I was hooked.

About the author

Kenneth Neal is a certified Enterprise Content Management Practitioner with over 20 years of corporate communications experience implementing programs for companies such as IBM, BearingPoint, Fujitsu Consulting and Canon Business Process Services, Inc. Ken has published articles on document management topics in such publications as *Business Solutions*, *Information Management*, *E-Document News*, and *Workflow*. He has also presented seminars at the New York Real Estate Institute, National Council on Economic Education, and ARMA (Association of Records Managers and Administrators). Ken's presentations at ARMA conventions have focused on mastering key forms of business communication including written, verbal and formal presentations.

Introduction: why communication skills for records and information managers?

"You can have brilliant ideas, but if you can't get them across, they won't get you anywhere."

(Lee Iacocca)

Communication counts. The rest of this book basically expands on this idea and offers suggestions on how to communicate effectively. My special focus is that communication counts particularly for records and information managers. Why these two groups of professionals? Because records and communication managers have to communicate a complex idea: namely, that their programs can help the organization succeed. If you are a records manager and you can't clearly get across why implementing a records retention schedule is critical, chances are that your proposal will be passed over. If you are an IT manager, and you haven't strategically communicated sound business reasons for your organization to improve its website, your initiative may come to a quick end.

Communication drives success

Successful records and information managers understand that effective communication helps them achieve better results because, beyond enabling the ability to clearly get across complex ideas, effective communication ultimately drives financial performance and overall business success.

Watson Wyatt Worldwide's Communication ROI Study asserts that effective internal communications benefits companies in a number of ways (Demitropoulos, 2010). These include keeping employees better engaged in the business, helping companies retain key talent, providing consistent value to customers, and delivering superior financial performance to shareholders. A key finding of the study was that organizations that communicate well had a 47 percent higher total return to shareholders over the last five years, compared with firms that are the least effective at communication.

In addition to enhancing business performance, records and information managers who are seen as true leaders also know another "secret" about communication: it boosts the morale of their teams. A survey developed by Accountemps®, a specialized staffing service for temporary accounting and finance professionals, found that better and more frequent communication with staff members is one of the best ways to raise employee morale (Demitropoulos, 2010). As you might suspect, the survey also found the opposite to be true. The absence of open and honest communication with staff tops the list of management mistakes that can wear down employee morale.

These findings indicate that the ability to effectively communicate is more than a skill; it is a powerful tool for records and information professionals. Using this tool they can more easily clarify the strategic value of their departments and programs, increase motivation and the efficiency of their teams and ultimately help sharpen their company's competitiveness.

Effectively communicating is more challenging than ever

One more reason I believe communication counts is because doing it effectively, whether in business or your personal life, is more challenging than ever. It's tempting not to worry about communicating effectively because to do so requires concentration and awareness. Most of all it requires attention – in the midst of a mind-boggling array of daily activities, events, information and people that constantly compete for your attention. Here's just one eye-opening statistic. According to a 2011 *Forbes* magazine article (Malone, 2011), in the 1970s people were exposed to about 500 commercial messages per day. Factoring in today's technology, that estimate has exploded to about 30,000 messages per day. Let's pause and take that in for a second – just today, 30,000 messages are vying to enter your consciousness.

And while you're trying to manage those 30,000 messages, what else are you trying to juggle during your day? According to a 2011 Bureau of Labor

Statistics report (USDL, 2011), if you're between 25 and 54 years of age with children your average 24-hour day consists of the following major activities: working (8.8 hours), sleeping (7.6 hours), leisure and sports (2.5 hours), caring for others (1.2 hours), eating and drinking (1.1 hours), household activities (1.1 hours) and other (1.7 hours). Let's add to the mix that while engaged in these activities you might also be managing email, texting, live chatting, tweeting, blogging, downloading, surfing (most likely the web, not the ocean) and talking on the phone, just to name a few. And if you're a records or information manager, you're probably also reading thousands if not millions of words each week while trying to absorb and manage countless documents and terabytes of information.

It's easy to consider why many of us are just too exhausted to focus on improving our communication skills. Yet, as these demands on our attention will certainly continue to grow and challenge our ability to communicate effectively, what is the alternative? If we don't communicate our brilliant ideas clearly, as Lee Iacocca points out, our ideas are not likely to get us anywhere.

The solution: six simple skills

The good news as I see it is that by honing six relatively simple skills, records and information managers, as well as everyone else, can more easily reap the business benefits I pointed out earlier.

Why six skills, and not seven or ten? The answer to this question is based on the many years I have spent directing internal and external communications programs for technology companies, giving presentations, proposing initiatives to senior executives, writing articles, press releases, case histories and many other forms of content. At one point in my career I began receiving invitations to lecture at seminars and industry conferences on how records and information managers can advance their professional lives by improving their writing and verbal skills. These groups, particularly records managers, compete for a slice of the corporate budget pie and, as I pointed out earlier, are challenged to communicate the complex idea of how their programs help drive organizational success.

When I began planning my first presentations, my goal was to craft a workable number of skills that my audience could easily remember. I also wanted my presentations to be more than just technical discussions.

I wanted them to be personal, linked with stories and examples of how these skills assisted me as well as colleagues and friends in advancing our careers and lives. Finally, I wanted these skills to function together, as a system, adding up to much more that any one skill individually. Implemented together, they provide a powerful persuasive force that greatly increases your chance of getting what you want. Eliminate just one skill during a presentation and that force is significantly diminished.

For example, imagine in a presentation to senior management you apply five of the skills but you're not coming across as credible. Your audience is not convinced that you know your stuff, that your records management proposal doesn't appear to be backed by any industry trends or a relevant case history example of how an effective records program helped a company avoid serious risk. Without credibility, the other five skills may not be enough to help you win the day.

Considering these and other elements, I eventually decided to focus on six skills in my first presentation. The number was workable, functioned well as a system, and based on my personal experience represented "the best of the best" in terms of getting results. Consequently, the six skills have been with me in my career, and in my professional life ever since. Now, I hope they will help support your professional journey as well.

In the first six chapters, I will focus on each of the skills: be brief, be clear, be responsive, be strategic and be credible. By including case history examples, personal events and stories from colleagues I will take the skills out of the realm of the theoretical and into the realm of the practical. You can start implementing each skill right away, perhaps as you write your next report or plan your next presentation.

The business case

In the seventh chapter I will highlight one of the most practical applications of applying the skills for records and information managers – the business case. I end with the business case because it is a critical document for records and information managers who want to win support for their programs. While records managers often don't have a chance to attain the status of a hero, here's one brief example of how a manager wrote a good business case, received budget approval by arguing for the project persuasively and then implemented the program, which saved his company substantial money.

The records manager, who worked for a food company, created a business case for a program that would help protect the organization against superfund problems. (A superfund site, according to the 1980 Comprehensive Environmental Response, Compensation, and Liability Act, is a toxic site placed on a list of sites requiring cleanup mandated by the Environmental Protection Agency.) The records manager went before the company's senior leadership team and basically argued: "The program I'm proposing will cost the company $10,000 but it will help us sleep better at night because we'll be better prepared if we ever face a superfund problem."

The issue, of which senior management was aware, was that the company had a mass of boxes containing insurance contracts that could protect the organization against future insurance claims. The insurance contracts, however, had never been indexed or inventoried. The program designed by the records manager would fix this problem. Sure enough, soon after the program was approved and implemented, the company was sued for a superfund cleanup. Because the company's records were now organized, the records manager was able to produce a contract, dated from 1942 and still in effect, that held the company harmless from the particulars in the lawsuit. The insurance company paid the fine, which totaled between $4 and $5 million dollars. Keep this story in the back of your mind as the "records manager and the superfund example." I'll return to it in future chapters. Besides being persuasive, it illustrates several other key communication skills.

Meeting the challenge

Writing and communicating a good business case doesn't always produce such a dramatic outcome. It is, however, critical for getting records and IT programs implemented that can help a company reduce costs and risk as well as streamline operations. While an effective business case embodies all the communication skills we'll be examining, it also represents a challenge for many professionals, not just records and information managers.

Let's move ahead and meet that challenge together.

Be brief: how brief?

"I will be brief. Not nearly so brief as Salvador Dali, who gave the world's shortest speech. He said, 'I will be so brief I have already finished,' and he sat down."

(Edward O. Wilson)

Abstract: Being brief can add power and clarity to your writing. While there are no strict rules or one formula for being brief, there are guidelines. One is to keep in mind examples of great speeches or presentations, such as the Gettysburg Address or Ernest Hemingway's six-word story, that are memorable because they said what needed to be said with relatively few words. The Flesch Reading Ease Score is another way to more quantitatively assess how difficult it is to read a section of text. With these guidelines in mind, two best practices for being brief in written and verbal communication include cutting extraneous words and writing as if you are talking to a friend.

Key words: brevity in writing, readability, Flesch Reading Ease Score, cut extraneous words, best practices for being brief, six-word challenge.

While the opening quote about Salvador Dali is one of my favorites, I'm not suggesting you use it as a model for your next executive presentation. It does, however, make an important point. Being brief can add power and clarity to your written and spoken words. Being brief can increase your chances of getting your message across – and your proposals accepted.

Guidelines for brevity

There's no strict formula for being brief. Every document, speech or presentation you deliver will be unique within the context of the situation. One guideline I follow is to remember that Abraham Lincoln's Gettysburg Address was a masterpiece of brevity. One of the most famous speeches in American history, it totaled 270 words. Few people remember that it was so brief because he said what needed to be said with great eloquence and few words, and then he sat down.

Recalling the context of the speech is enlightening. The Battle of Gettysburg was a bloody victory for the Union, resulting in the death of more than 45,000 soldiers. The battle also marked the beginning of the end of the Confederacy. America needed its president to offer words that could help foster healing and encourage peace.

Lincoln, however, was not the main speaker that day at the dedication of the cemetery. The keynote address was given by the famous orator Edward Everett. He delivered a speech of 13,500 words that took about two hours – 50 times the length of Lincoln's speech. Yet it was Lincoln's words that took their place in history.

There is another guideline I follow that helps me remember the power of brevity. As recounted in the play, *Papa*, Ernest Hemingway claims that he won $10 by meeting a challenge to write a story in six words. What were those six words? "For sale. Baby shoes. Never worn." I'm willing to bet that the six words just elicited some feelings.

There are variations of the "six-word challenge" to this day. Two years ago, a *New York Times* blog column published an article about the results of "The Six-Word Memoir Contest" (Parker-Pope, 2011). Readers were challenged to explain their mother, someone else's mother or motherhood in general in six words. The contest drew 7000 submissions. Six winners were featured in the blog column. Here are three of the winning six-word memoirs that I particularly like:

> Not entirely happy until completely discontent.
> Friends finally. But not on Facebook.
> She deserves more than six words.

The six-word challenge is a great and fun way to practice brevity in writing. You might try challenging yourself as well as your records or IT staff. For example, imagine I was a member of your records management staff and you challenged the team to explain why an effective records management program is important. I might focus on the risk reduction benefits of records management and submit this: "Good records. Program tight. Sleep tonight." Give it a try; you may enjoy the challenge and at the same time gain a new appreciation for the power of brevity.

It's not easy being brief

Yet despite the Gettysburg Address, Hemingway's very short story, the six-word memoir contest and many other examples I can cite, all of us are continuously challenged to be brief, particularly in our writing. In the book *Why Business Peoples Speak like Idiots* (Fugere et al., 2005),[1] the authors offer an interesting take on the reason for what they humorously refer to as "document obesity:"

> "There's a reason we get beat up with hour-long presentations and four-minute voicemails with endings that no one ever listens to. Length implies that some work went into the production. It takes time to write 50 pages about something, but if we turn in five pages, it looks as though we haven't put much time into the job.
>
> High school teachers use this technique. A term paper must be 20 pages and have two pages of footnotes, from at least five different sources. In some ways, this is a useful guideline for high school students who might have no way of knowing how many pages it would take to cover topic X. It also weeds out the students who don't want to do any real work, because it's (slightly) easier to crank out five pages of garbage than 15 pages.
>
> But guidelines like these are not so useful in the business world where the objective isn't to spend a minimum amount of 12 hours in the library. The objective is to connect, convince, and make money."

Make your writing more readable

While these and other examples might be helpful, there's another guideline that provides a more quantitative way to think about how to make your writing more readable. The Flesch Reading Ease Score and the Flesch–Kincaid Reading Grade Level measure your writing's readability. Basically, these tests provide a method to calculate the difficulty of reading a section of text, as measured by the education level required of the reader.

Dr. Rudolph Flesch developed his Flesch Reading Ease Score in 1946. It is based on a complex formula that tallies what he called a document's readability score. The scores are plotted on a scale of 0 to 100, with 100 being the easiest to read. (It is next to impossible to write something that scores 100 outside of possibly "See spot run.") Table 1.1 offers some examples that show Flesch Readability Scores in practice.

| **Table 1.1** | Flesch Readability Scores in practice |

Publication	Flesch Readability Score
Comic books	92
Sports Illustrated magazine	63
Wall Street Journal	43
The IRS Tax Code	−6

What you may find surprising is that the average person reads and comprehends – and is therefore most likely to be persuaded – at about the 6th and 7th grade reading level. If copywriters keep their written content within a Flesch Reading Ease Score of 60–70 (the reading ability of an average 13 to 15-year-old student), they are more likely to reach, satisfy, convince and convert the greatest amount of people.[2]

The Flesch Reading Ease Score, which takes into account sentence and word length, indicates sentences longer than 21 words prove challenging and that when the average syllable count of words in a given text approaches two, reading ease declines. Compare the following examples:

It was decided that the gymnasium be locked after the institution's operating hours in an effort to thwart the local vandals' destruction. (Flesch Reading Ease 38.3; Flesch-Kincaid Grade Level 12.0)

with

To stop the vandalism at the gym, Mr. Brown decided to keep it locked after school. (Flesch Reading Ease 82.2; Flesch-Kincaid Grade level 5.7; McGahan, 2013)

Three best practices for being brief

1. Cut extraneous words

According to the Flesch Reading Ease Score, short sentences are more memorable than long ones. Keeping this in mind, one best practice to ensure you maximize readability is to cut extraneous words. Keeping sentences within a maximum of 18 words is a good rule of thumb. Here is an example:

Before   This year, after a careful fine-tuning of our records management budget, we were able to reduce our program costs by a grand total of $30,000 (26 words).

After   This year we saved $30,000 in records management program costs (10 words).

How do you decide what words are extraneous and can be cut? Here's a way to start. The classic writing style manual, *The Elements of Style* by William Strunk and E.B. White states that "the fact that," "who is" and "which was" are the most commonly used needless words. Instead of the first phrase you can use a single word and for the latter two you can simply omit them. Here are examples:

Before   Because of the fact that people benefitted from reading my book, I decided to follow up with another.

After   Because people benefitted from reading my book, I wrote another.

Before   Cheryl, who is an information technology consultant, is a knowledgeable person.

After   Cheryl, an information technology consultant, is a knowledgeable person.

Before   The proposal, which was written by Cheryl, was well received.

After   Cheryl's proposal was well received.

2. Use one-syllable words

The second best practice is to use one-syllable words as often as possible. Just as short sentences can add impact to your communication, one-syllable words can build momentum and give the long ones impact. A fine example of this principle is Winston Churchill, particularly his speech to the House of Commons on 4 June 1940.

Like the Gettysburg Address, people needed their leader to say words that would help them through a challenging time. In this speech, Churchill had to describe a great military disaster, and warn of a possible invasion attempt by Nazi Germany, while encouraging faith in eventual victory.

In the excerpt below, the majority of his words are one syllable. He uses those plain words, however, to create a momentum and power that are unforgettable. And though he breaks the rule of thumb I just previously highlighted about sentence length – his first sentence contains 42 words, his second 33 – he does so in a way that undeniably works:

"We shall go on to the end, we shall fight in France, we shall fight on the seas and oceans, we shall fight with growing confidence and growing strength in the air, we shall defend our island, whatever the cost may be. We shall fight on the beaches, we shall fight on the landing grounds, we shall fight in the fields and in the streets, we shall fight in the hills; we shall never surrender."

3. Write as if talking to a friend

The third best practice is one I use often use when I'm stuck on a sentence. Step back from your computer and ask yourself the question, "How can I write this as if I'm talking to a friend?" Asking this question can help steer you away from a tangled web of words and toward plain English. In many of my presentations to records and IT managers I underscore this approach by pointing (with humor) to the legal field as an example of how not to write as if talking to a friend. Legal language is often exasperating to those of us who are not lawyers precisely because it seems to avoid plain English, preferring endlessly long sentences peppered with vaguely Latin-sounding phrases.

Peter Tiersma in his article "The nature of legal language"[3] gives an example that drives the point home. Table 1.2 compares a typical modern will written in legal language, totaling 84 words, with the same will written in plain English, totaling 27 words.

To write as if talking to a friend, I suggest two things. First, write without editing a word. Let it flow. I see this as a right-brain, creative process. The left brain will take care of spelling, punctuation, grammar and eliminating unnecessary words later. At this point, don't think of what you're doing as "writing." Consider it "brainstorming" or whatever word you choose to describe the process. Just keep the words moving across the page as if you are thinking out loud and sharing your thoughts with a friend or co-worker over a cup of coffee. I like the way Jane Watson, in her book *Business Writing Basics*, puts it:

"When you pause to search for the best phrase or sentence, you halt the right brain's activities and let the left brain take over. What would

Table 1.2   Legal will versus plain English

Typical modern will (84 words)	What it really says (27 words)
I give, devise and bequeath all of rest, residue and remainder of my property which I may own at the time of my death, real, personal and mixed, of whatsoever kind and nature and wheresoever situate, including all property which I may acquire or to which I may become entitled after the execution of this will, in equal shares, absolutely and forever, to ARCHIE SMITH, LUCY SMITH, his wife, and ARCHIBALD SMITH, per capita, to any of them living ninety days after my death	I give the rest of my estate in equal shares to Archie Smith, Lucy Smith, and Archibald Smith, assuming they survive me by at least 90 days

happen if you tried to drive a car with your feet on the brake and the gas pedal at the same time? The ride would be jerky and your progress slow. Why operate your brain this way? When you write and edit at the same time, you only slow yourself down. Remember the golden rule for writers: First write it; then make it right."

(Watson, 2007)

This flowing, non-edited form of writing may take five minutes, an hour or more depending on the content you're composing, such as an email, a paragraph in a report, a section of a case history or the introduction to a white paper. When you finish your current writing session, put the pen down or save and close the document, and walk away for a while. The time pressure to finish your document will determine how long you can rest before the first edit. If it's a critical email that must be completed and sent in the next half hour, for example, you might have only a few minutes to take a break, but take it. If you just drafted a section of a report that is due in a few weeks, and you're on track to finish the report on time, take an hour before coming back and doing the first edit.

Notice I say the "first edit." Ideally I suggest editing a section of text at least three times, always with a break in between. The pressure of a deadline dictates the editing process but if time allows I always follow this "three edit rule," keeping in mind that I want my final result to sound as if I'm talking to a friend. This doesn't mean I have to only use one-syllable words and every single sentence has to be extremely brief. It means that by editing for brevity – as well as for the other five keys such as clarity and persuasiveness, which I will cover in later chapters – I have maximized the chance that my writing will achieve its goal.

Many writers, me included, initially regard editing as "work" and eventually learned to like and even love the process. One analogy is that of a sculptor at work.

With each session of chipping away pieces of stone, a work of art emerges.

I'll conclude this chapter with an example I offered when I presented a seminar at the national conference of the Association of Records Managers and Administrators (ARMA). Prior to the conference, I had written a short paragraph describing how I realized my dream of achieving an opportunity to present at the ARMA conference. In my example I highlighted the first draft of the paragraph, written without editing and the result after thee edits.

Ken had a dream of speaking at ARMA. His boss agreed that doing more industry presentations was a good performance goal for this year. Ken then drafted a proposal and sent it to ARMA. The ARMA education committee approved Ken's presentation, which ultimately enabled him to meet his performance goal. (Three sentences, 50 words)

Supported by his boss, Ken met his performance goal and realized his dream of speaking at ARMA by drafting a proposal that was approved by the association. (One sentence, 27 words)

I explained to my audience that my final version had eliminated many extraneous words, incorporated one-syllable words when appropriate and sounded more like I was talking to a friend. Consequently the second version demanded much less work to understand the story.

The first version presented the story in series of steps spanning three sentences (i.e., had a dream, obtained boss's agreement, drafted a proposal, sent it to ARMA, etc.). This requires my audience to spend more time and effort to absorb the full story compared with the final, concise version.

Audiences, particularly business executives, always appreciate it when they don't have to work hard to understand your message because you've taken the time to be concise. They also like it when you communicate as clearly as possible, a skill I'll address in the next chapter.

Notes

1. I also drew from Fugere et al.'s comments about the power and brevity of Lincoln's Gettysburg Address versus Everett's speech at the dedication of the cemetery.
2. Jen McGahan, "Flesch Reading Ease: seven copywriting tips that keep people reading." Retrieved 11 April 2013 from *http://myteamconnects.com/flesch-reading-ease-seven-copywriting-tips-that-keep-people-reading/* While McGahan's article focuses on copywriting tips, her suggestions, such as using short punchy words and action words, are just as useful for writing business proposals and presentations.
3. Peter Tiersma, "The nature of legal language." Retrieved 16 April 2013 from *http://www.languageandlaw.org/NATURE.HTM*

Be clear: is my proposal full of jargon?

"I notice that you use plain, simple language, short words, and brief sentences. That is the way to write English – it is the modern way and the best way. Stick to it; don't let fluff and the flowers and verbosity creep in."

(Mark Twain)

Abstract: Using unclear language filled with jargon, vague words and cliché phrases that have been uttered or written countless times before exposes records and information managers to a risk. By boring or alienating their audience with stale presentations, their message will be ignored. Proposals and budgets will be denied. Information managers can avoid falling into this trap by following a few simple guidelines and learning to ask four questions that will enable them to tailor their communication to the needs of their audience. This approach significantly raises the chances for success.

Key words: jargon, clichés, buzzwords, George Orwell, William Zinsser, acronyms, persuasion, likability, fuzzy language, Plain English Campaign, legal language.

The opening quote in this chapter offers a great description of clarity in writing. And who can argue with Mark Twain? He did write a few classics and sell a few books. If he was alive today and working in the corporate world I doubt that he would engage in what I refer to as "business speak." My definition of business speak is language that pretends to communicate, but doesn't. It's language that tries to make the negative appear positive. It's language that avoids responsibility. It's language that instead of clarifying a point of view, evades it.

The fuzziness of language

Let's take a simple example. A doll is a doll, correct? Yet when Mattel started to import GI Joe action figures, U.S. customs officials weren't amused. These are dolls and subject to the import tariff on dolls, said the customs officials. No, replied Mattel, these are action figures. Boys don't play with dolls, so these can't be dolls but must be action figures. After an eight-year court battle Mattel lost, but of course still labels GI Joe as an action figure in its advertising (Lutz, 1996)[1].

So is Joe a doll or an action figure? Joe is what we decide to call him. For the courts Joe is a doll. For Mattel and the boys who play with him, Joe is an action figure. This disagreement about labeling Joe has to do with a problem inherent in language, a problem that linguists and writers sometimes refer to as "fuzziness." It's a common problem we all experience because any word we select to describe a thing or event is doomed to be inadequate. The reason is that the word we choose cannot truly represent the complex reality we are trying to describe. It can only represent our perception of reality, not what exists. This is why many business executives resort, consciously or unconsciously, to deploying one of the great enemies of clear communication: jargon.

Jargon is technical language. There's nothing wrong with it if the language is appropriate for the intended audience. Even with that caveat, I suggest avoiding jargon as much as possible. Why? Because eliminating jargon helps avoid confusing your audience and improves the possibility that your message is being clearly received. For example, you might get by using the word "iterative" if you're in engineering. I suggest using "frequent." If you work in the healthcare industry, using the word "efficacy" might not raise eyebrows. Alternatively, I would go with "effectiveness."

A sea of acronyms and jargon

Years ago I was hired as a communications manager for one of the world's technology leaders, a giant in software, hardware, research and information technology services. Up until that time, I had worked for small and medium-sized public relations firms, specializing in consumer electronics and technology accounts. Somewhat naively, I expected to make the job transition easily.

I quickly discovered, however, that I was entering a new business culture that had its own language. My new boss invited me to a departmental staff meeting that was scheduled a few days before I officially began work. This would offer me an opportunity to meet some key people and start to become acquainted with the technology and services I would be promoting.

That morning I sat down, opened my notebook, clicked my pen and was ready to take notes in preparation for my new professional adventure. An executive opened the meeting with an in-depth presentation on the company's strategic direction and planned new services offerings. After about 15 minutes, I hadn't written one word in my notebook. The reason: I didn't understand anything the presenter was talking about. Despite my background, I was quickly drowning in a sea of technology terms, acronyms and jargon, none of which was clear to me. I continued to nod my head knowingly as the presenter rattled on about ISPs, VPNs, GUIs, ISDN, client/server configurations and peer-to-peer networks.

One jargon phrase was particularly baffling, mysterious and in the context of the presentation began to take on a science fiction–like aura in my mind. The presenter kept referring to "the glass house." I wondered about the glass house. What was it? Where was it located? Why was it made of glass? What was in it? I could have simply asked someone what this phrase meant, but I didn't want to appear unprofessional.

Eventually I did ask and learned that there was nothing mystical about the glass house. At that time it referred to large windowed rooms that contained mainframe computers and other hardware devices necessary for data storage and processing. Today the term refers generally to the centrally administered computing environments of enterprises. As computers have gotten smaller and can be fit into smaller spaces, they are no longer housed in centralized rooms surrounded by glass windows. However, the term "glass house" is still used to describe an organization's centrally controlled computing environment. I often think of that meeting and the ominous-sounding "glass house" when I'm tempted to use jargon. Yes, it was appropriate for the audience in the room that morning. But if my goal is to clearly communicate something about mainframe computer environments to a general business audience, I'll opt for plain language. It lowers the risk that my readers will feel the same way I did that morning.

Straight talk and likability

Using jargon and fuzzy language in order to sound impressive or to try and make something unpleasant sound more acceptable exposes you to another risk. Your audience may become irritated with you. This is important. In his book *The Power of Persuasion*, Robert Levine, a professor of psychology states:

> "If you could master just one element of professional communication that is more powerful than anything ... it is the quality of being likable. I call it the magic bullet, because if your audience likes you, they'll forgive just about everything else you do wrong. If they don't like you, you can hit every rule right on target and it doesn't matter."
>
> (Levine, 2003).

Yet despite this critical link between straight talking and likability, organizations often choose to couch their messages in vague, obscure and jargon-laden language that could only be described in the same words Harry Belafonte used in a song about a confusing explanation: "It was clear as mud but it covered the ground."

Is it worth the effort to be clear and straightforward? In *Why Business People Speak like Idiots*, authors Brian Fugere, Chelsea Hardaway and Jon Warshawsky put this question to the test in what they call their "Starbucks study" (Fugere et al., 2005). They chose an Atlanta Starbucks to research the effect that obscure writing had on people. The approach was simple. Show everyday people two writing samples, one filled with jargon and business speak and one that used straightforward and clear language. The names of the companies associated with the writing samples were not disclosed. People participating in the survey were asked to rate each sample according to 30 common psychological traits, 15 "good" (such as friendly) and 15 "bad" (such as rude). Following are excerpts of the two writing samples (see Table 2.1):

As you might have guessed, the Starbucks patrons didn't like sample 1, the "obscure" annual report, associating it with traits such as *obnoxious*, *rude, stubborn* and *unreliable*. It's not a stretch to imagine that people would also associate these traits with a writer or speaker of similar content. That's the serious risk each of us takes when we communicate in this manner. Results for writing sample 2, the "straight talk" annual report, were much more positive. People selected traits including *likable, energetic, friendly, inspiring* and *enthusiastic*. None of the 15 "bad" traits were associated with the annual report that used clear, straightforward language.

According to the study, if you want to be likable to your audience, which in turn increases your chance of persuasively getting your message across, clarity is the way to go.

Table 2.1   The Starbucks Study

Writing sample 1 (annual report)	Writing Sample 2 (annual report)
Since the foundation of an agency's IT portfolio is its infrastructure, it behooves an IT-savvy council to elevate infrastructure decisions to the enterprise level. Historically, CIOs have had difficulty getting the attention of executives on this critical issue because infrastructure is usually described in terms of technology components rather than in terms of business capability. The purpose of building an enterprise IT infrastructure is to enable the sharing of information and expensive resources while creating a mechanism for cross-unit service delivery and economies of scale	In many ways, ABC company is not a normal store. We have a deep selection that is unconstrained by shelf space. We turn our inventory 19 times a year. We personalize the store for each and every customer. We trade real estate for technology (which gets cheaper and more capable every year). We display customer reviews critical of our products. You can make a purchase within a few seconds and one click. We put used products next to new ones so you can choose. We share our prime real estate – our product detail pages – with third parties, and, if they can offer better value, we let them

While successfully promoting the growth of records and information management programs requires serious commitment and energy, the Starbucks study is a lighthearted way of reminding us that clear communication is a critical element of meeting these and other business goals.

Retaining a sense of humanity

Author William Zinsser emphasizes that clarity in writing is not just a question of likability, but of retaining a sense of humanity, of warmth in your communication. While reminding us that most people work for institutions, he makes the following important points.

"But just because people work for an institution, they don't have to write like one. Institutions can be warmed up. Administrators can be turned into human beings. Information can be imparted clearly and without pomposity. You only have to remember that people identify with people, not with abstractions like 'profitability,' or with Latinate nouns like 'utilization' and 'implementation,' or with inert constructions in which nobody can be visualized doing something: 'pre-feasibility studies are in the paperwork stage'."

Still, plain talk will not be easily achieved in corporate America. Too much vanity is on the line. Managers at every level are prisoners of the notion that a simple style reflects a simple mind. Actually a simple style is the result of hard work and hard thinking; a muddled style reflects a muddled thinker or a person too arrogant, or too dumb, or too lazy to organize his thoughts. Remember that what you write is often the only chance you'll get to present yourself to someone whose business or money or goodwill you need. If what you write is ornate, or pompous, or fuzzy, that's how you'll be perceived. The reader has no other choice (Zinsser, 2006).[2]

A campaign for plain English

I imagine Zinsser would applaud (if he hasn't already) an organization entirely dedicated to clarity in communication, the U.K.-based Plain English Campaign.[3] The Campaign's website states that it has been "fighting for crystal-clear communication since 1979." The organization's mission is to help correct what it calls "gobbledygook, jargon and misleading public information." In this effort it helps government departments and other official organizations bring clarity to their documents, reports and publications. The Campaign believes that everyone should have access to clear and concise information.

The initiative officially began after founder Chrissie Maher OBE[4] publicly shredded hundreds of official documents in Parliament Square, London. While the Campaign often shares its viewpoint with a sense of humor, its goal is serious: to help ensure that the U.K. government and other organizations communicate public information as clearly as possible.

One element of the Campaign that I find particularly interesting is its Crystal Mark, a seal of approval for the clarity of a document. It now appears on over 21,000 different documents in the U.K., the U.S.A., Australia, Denmark, New Zealand and South Africa. It is the only internationally recognized mark of its kind. If you're wondering how the Campaign defines clarity, here it is: "The only measure of a document's clarity is whether it can be read, understood and acted upon in a single reading." For records and information managers, and anyone who aspires to clear communication, this is a definition worth remembering.

Governmental and business organizations that don't share the Campaign's dedication to clarity risk winning its annual Golden Bull "worst written nonsense" award. Here is one winner of a 2012 Golden Bull, an organization named Transport for London, for its explanation of a "billing period:"

> "Billing Period in relation to CC Auto Pay means a period of 1 month or such other period as Transport for London may determine and specify on its Congestion Charging website in each case beginning with the day on which Transport for London accepts an application for the Registration of a CC Auto Pay Account or such other day as Transport for London may in the particular circumstances of the case accept. First Billing Period may be shorter than 1 month dependent on what day of the month is selected for statement generation."

The Campaign underscores its point in other ways, including a playful resource it calls the "gobbledygook generator." Simply click on a button that states "generate some gobbledygook" and a random piece of business jargon will appear in the box below the button. If you need more than one buzz phrase, just can click the button again and again. Clicking the button twice yielded the following buzz phrases:

> "Our upgraded model now offers parallel third-generation paradigm shifts. We need to get on-message about our systemized reciprocal time-phases."

Many of us in business and government might cringe a bit reading these phrases. We know how close we've come countless times to writing such jargon-laden sentences that have enveloped our readers in a fog of words that don't point to any meaningful conclusion. The good news is that the Campaign's message is being heard, and promoted, by some of the world's most influential leaders and communicators. Here's a statement on the Campaign's website by British Prime Minister David Cameron:

> "All politicians are guilty of slipping into jargon – and all of us deserve scrutiny from the Plain English Campaign. Complicated sets of initials, official jargon, bureaucracies that over-complicate things to boost their own self-importance – all of these things help to build barriers between government and people. When important information is being provided by officials or government departments – that is especially serious. So I congratulate the Campaign on all it has achieved to date, and wish it well."

Your job has been "demised"

Jargon not only builds barriers between governments and people, as the Prime Minister points out, it can build barriers between businesses and people. This is especially the case when an organization uses jargon in order to be deliberately evasive. A prime example is when a large number of employees are fired – except they are rarely "fired" anymore or even "laid off." The latest euphemism, reported by *The Times* of London, referred to announcement by HSBC that it was cutting more than a thousand jobs in the wake of new rules on advising customers. According to *The Times*: "The bank said yesterday that it would 'demise' many of the jobs, bringing a new word for sacking into the corporate lexicon" (Wright, 2013).

There are, however, other ways you can lose your job besides having it "demised." You can become "redundant," "excessed," "transitioned," offered "voluntary severance" or subjected to a "focused reduction." Your job can be declared "excess to requirements," which means that you haven't been laid off, just that your job has been eliminated. Here is one of my personal favorite examples as described by author William Lutz:

> "However, I think the winner for best doublespeak for firing comes from the computer industry, where you're not fired; you're "uninstalled." Call a vice president at this company and the voice mail message will tell you that "you have reached the number of an uninstalled vice president." I'm sure we all hope he gets installed some place real soon."
>
> (Lutz, 1996)

Many sources like the Plain English Campaign offer numerous samples of unclear, evasive writing that is virtually impossible to understand. I heartily recommend taking the time to read these samples and click buttons on any of the jargon, buzzword and gobbledygook generators available on the Internet as often as possible. This practice can work wonders in reminding you to compose your next document in plain English. Your readers will greatly appreciate being able to, paraphrasing the Campaign, "read, understand and act upon your document in a single reading."

Put clichés in the delete folder

Jargon, buzzwords and fuzzy language aren't the only challenges to communicating clearly. Besides avoiding these bad habits, eliminating clichés is a best practice that can help bring clarity to the written and spoken word. By cliché I am going beyond a strict definition to include any word, phrase or metaphor that is so overused it has become meaningless, unable any more to underscore an idea by evoking a visual image or eliciting an emotional response.

The best writing and verbal presentations incorporate words that were selected carefully for their meaning and to clearly communicate what the person wants to say. On the other hand, phrases such as "permit me to say ..." or "it all boils down to ..." are meaningless filler. An effective way to put your audience in a state of confusion (or boredom) is to combine these types of worn phrases with "legalese" such as "hereto" or "hereinafter." Here is a joke that illustrates this point:

> After months of bickering, a divorce lawyer completes negotiations with the other side and calls his client with the good news.
>
> "So what did you work out?" George asks the lawyer.
>
> "Well, what it boils down to is that the party of the first part, to wit, George Smith, shall convey to the party of the second part and to her heirs and assigns forever fee simple to the matrimonial estate, including all property real and person and all chattels appurtenant thereto."
>
> "I don't get any of that," George muttered.
>
> "That's right," said the lawyer.

At the end of the day, I suggest you visualize putting stale phrases that everyone else has used a million times, such as "at the end of the day ..." and legalese language into a mental "delete folder." Periodically empty all contents from the folder. The result will be that when writing a proposal or crafting a presentation, you'll have to invent new phrases to get your point across. This is a good thing because it will make you stand out. It will give you persuasive power.

One of the best essays ever written that offers insight and suggested rules to avoid using cliché-ridden language is George Orwell's "Politics and the English Language," written in 1946 (Orwell, 2002). The essay is as relevant now as it was then.

As Orwell points out, writers strip their passages of power and precision when they become lazy and almost indifferent as to whether their words mean anything or not.

"As soon as certain topics are raised, the concrete melts into the abstract and no one seems able to think of turns of speech that are not hackneyed:

prose consists less of *words* chosen for the sake of their meaning, and more and more of *phrases* tacked together like the sections of a prefabricated henhouse."

(Orwell, 2002)

One way to avoid the scenario Orwell describes is to choose each word carefully, making sure it has a purpose. The best business writing, from emails to comprehensive new business proposals, is economical. All unnecessary words are eliminated and the words that remain are precision tools that yield clear expression. This is in contrast to, paraphrasing Orwell, writing that is no more than a stream of clichés, dead metaphors and pretentious diction that relies on words such as *phenomenon* and *categorical* to dress up simple statements, giving an air of scientific impartiality to biased judgments. With this approach you increase your chances of not being liked as well as the probability that your audience will fall into a self-hypnotic trance or start longing for happy hour.

Avoid focusing on yourself

One practice that I believe incorporates these and many other rules and guidelines for clear communication is to avoid focusing on yourself. Focus on your audience instead. Take a strategic approach by tailoring your content and delivery to their needs, not yours. You'll be far more persuasive. A fairly easy way to achieve this goal, which I emphasize in my presentations to information managers, is to ask four questions. Let's imagine you are a records manager preparing to present to a senior executive audience. The questions in Table 2.2 will help you organize your thoughts, find the right words and increase the odds you'll get what you want.

Perhaps by presenting a brief, clear and tailored message, you won the day and the senior executives opted to implement the records retention schedule. Now on to the next challenge.

In order to continue to win – by providing value to your organization and thriving in your career – you'll need to hone another communication skill. It's an ability that enables business professionals to adapt their persuasive talents to environments and executive agendas that constantly change. Yesterday's records and IT programs no longer meet the needs of the company today. The market shifts. Industry trends evolve.

Table 2.2   The four key questions

Question	Answer
What am I trying to achieve?	I want management to approve the budget and resources that will enable our department to implement a records retention schedule
How will my audience react to what I am trying to achieve?	They probably won't listen because they don't think my proposal is important
Will my message be resisted?	Yes because the company has other pressing priorities right now
What do I know about my audience that will help me tailor my message?	I know the senior executives don't want the company to be exposed to legal liability for failing to meet industry compliance and other regulations. This can enable me to help them understand the program's importance. How? One way is to highlight actual case history examples of what happened to organizations that did not implement adequate records retention schedules and as a result, encountered legal and financial difficulties that damaged their reputation

New laws, compliance regulations and best practices are established. A crisis requires the company to immediately take a fresh approach. These and other scenarios take place every day. To solve them, information managers need to listen, carefully, all the time. We'll examine this critical skill, which one author refers to as a "lost art," in the next chapter.

Notes

1. Lutz offers a variety of fascinating examples and anecdotes on how organizations manipulate language for business and political reasons as well as to evade the truth.
2. Zinsser's book is a classic on the subject. I read and re-read it periodically not only to continually learn, but for the pleasure of his writing.

3. Readers can learn about The Plain English Campaign at *www.plainenglish.co.uk* The website offers a wealth of interesting information, quotes and writing samples. The Campaign underscores its commitment to clear writing with a sense of humor, particularly in the form of its annual Golden Bull, Kick in the Pants and Foot in Mouth awards. It's hard to come away from the website without feeling a renewed dedication to clear, concise writing. In addition to humor, the Campaign also emphasizes the serious side of unclear communication. This includes, for example, how complex medical jargon and unclear diagnoses could put lives at risk. The Campaign cites a study that found that nearly half of working-age people in Great Britain cannot understand or use everyday health information, such as clearly understanding medicine label instructions or signs in hospitals. The Campaign stresses that for some people this situation could literally be a matter of life or death.

4. OBE stands for Order of the British Empire, an order of chivalry established by King George V in 1917.

Be receptive: am I asking questions and listening?

"Understanding is a two way street"   (Eleanor Roosevelt)

Abstract: Asking effective questions and listening intently to the answers provides a powerful "one-two" punch that can take communications effectiveness to a higher level. Being receptive in this way yields many advantages. Learning to ask more effective questions can help records and IT professionals gain valuable insights and data enabling them to be more successful in their projects and in their careers. Gaining better listening skills brings benefits such as being perceived more positively and the improved ability to be persuasive.

Key words: asking questions, effective listening techniques, American Listening Association, the answering reflex, challenges to listening, art of asking questions, company mission statement, persuasive communication, psychological air, strategic communication.

Communication is the most important skill in business. Without it, there would be no enterprise. The organization would have no valuable information upon which to thrive. No appealing products or services could be launched. No effective organizational business strategy could be implemented. Internal systems and processes would be in disarray. The foundation for effective business communication, which consistently yields important data that allow the organization to succeed, is to ask questions and listen very carefully – in a way few of us have been trained to do so.

They didn't even listen

Imagine you are experiencing pain in your left knee and decide to visit the doctor to get it taken care of. After a few minutes the doctor enters the examination room, crosses his arms and inquires about your problem. You start to relate your symptoms but in about 15 seconds the doctor interrupts you and hands over a prescription for a course of physical therapy to cure tendonitis – for your elbow.

"I've had tendonitis of the elbow and physical therapy has always worked for me," he says.

"But this can't possibly work!" you exclaim. "My pain is in my knee. Besides, you didn't ask any questions or really listen to what I was saying."

"What do you mean it can't work?" he responds. "I've had elbow problems before and physical therapy has always worked for me. Give it a try; I'm sure it will work for you."

"Doctor, it's my knee that is hurting and I need you to help me cure the pain."

"But I am trying. Why are you resisting my diagnosis and prescription? Your elbow will be as good as new in a few weeks."

Let's imagine another scenario. You are the director of the IT department of a large corporation. You begin a meeting with a key manager on your staff, explaining that you want him to head up a project to improve the company's intranet (its internal website). It's been more than ten years since the intranet was initially launched and its functionality, content and other elements are not meeting the current needs of the organization. Your IT manager smiles and says he has the solution.

"We'll implement a state-of-the-art collaborative software solution," he states.

"But our sales and operations people don't need a collaboration solution," you counter. "Initial feedback indicates they need better organized, updated content and a way to search for specific documents. Besides, you haven't done any internal research yet, asked our executives any questions and listened to their answers in order to verify our business needs and other functional requirements."

"We really don't need to ask any questions or initiate any internal research," he responds. "Years ago I managed an intranet update for a leading corporation and a new collaboration system worked fine. I'm sure that will be the case here. I'll get going on the project right away."

What are the chances that you'd have any confidence in the doctor or the IT manager? The answer is, probably very little. Why? Because they offered a solution before they even investigated the problem. They didn't ask questions. They didn't even listen.

The one-two punch

Asking questions and listening are what I often refer to as the "one-two punch" of effective communication. The Free Dictionary (*www.freedictionary.com*) provides an informal definition of "one-two punch" as "an especially forceful or effective combination or sequence of two things." Asking questions and listening is precisely that "effective combination" of two things that can dramatically increase your ability to get the job done and further your career.

Let's start with the first power punch – asking questions – and what better way to begin this topic than by ... asking a question. What are the risks for a records manager or IT professional who don't take the time to ask carefully considered questions? If you're a records manager, one of your responsibilities is to make sure your company is compliant with its records management policy and schedule. If you're not asking questions (and listening), you won't know what you should be doing in terms of problems and opportunities. Is everyone getting the information they need when they need it, from the receptionist to the c-level executive? If you're an IT manager, you need to be aware of complaints that the IT department is receiving. Perhaps the company website is not functioning properly or the network is suddenly too slow. Are you waiting until these and other problems get out of hand or are you proactively investigating by asking questions, listening to the answers, diagnosing the problems and implementing solutions quickly and effectively?

A records management nightmare

Bottom line, you can cause big problems by not asking the right question at the right time. Here's one true story of a records manager who failed to ask a few critical questions. A service provider put together a records retention schedule and a records management training program for a client that then suspended the project. The client implemented the retention schedule but never initiated the training.

The company then became involved in litigation spanning two states. Because the records manager didn't go through any training (which included preparing for legal discovery), she didn't ask a few critical questions such as "how are the documents relevant to the litigation going to be sent to me?" and "how should the documents be organized?" There was no planning process. The result: the company suddenly had ten pallets of boxes with legal documents that were literally dumped into the boxes with no folders, no dates and no form of organization.

The service provider had to be called back in to help the company sort and organize the documents. The records management chaos included the fact that several boxes were damp when documents were tossed into them and the documents became mildewed and stuck together. This is just one example in the records management arena of how asking the right questions at the right time could have helped the company avoid major problems.

This is the opposite of what happened in the "records manager and the superfund example" I highlighted in the introduction. In that case, the records manager did ask the right questions at the right time: "Are we prepared if we face a superfund lawsuit?" The answer was no. "What should we do to become prepared?" The answer was that the company should inventory and index its records. You remember the rest. The company was sued and because it had organized its records, it was prepared and avoided paying millions of dollars in fines.

Why we don't ask more questions

As these examples point out, asking questions has a number of important advantages, some of which I'll spotlight shortly. But first, despite these advantages, why don't we ask more questions? In her book *The 7 Powers of Questions: Secrets to Successful Communication in Life and at Work*,[1] author Dorothy Leeds highlights several reasons. One of the most common is being afraid to question authority. It sometimes seems easier to accept the word of someone you fear rather than face a confrontation.

Another reason is that questions can make us appear vulnerable. This can be a big issue in the business arena where most of us would rather appear that we have it all together, all the time. However, our need to ask a question is often greatest when we're most vulnerable. This includes when we're angry or upset. When the person we're dealing with is our boss or supervisor and we're afraid for our job. When we're in the presence of someone with specific knowledge, such as a doctor or lawyer, and we automatically assume they know best.

A third reason is that some of us have been brought up to think that asking questions is probing into someone's life and "nice people" don't do it. A string of questions can make someone feel like they're being interrogated. But that's not what we're talking about here – which is to establish a dialogue, a give and take, in a situation.

Questions encourage answers

Whatever challenges a records or IT manager may have for not asking questions, it would be worthwhile to overcome them because asking questions provides a critical business advantage – it encourages answers. One reason for this is what experts like Dorothy Leeds refer to as the "answering reflex" (Leeds, 2000). We have hundreds of reflexes like blinking at a loud noise. There is also an answering reflex. When a question is asked, we feel it must be answered, even if not out loud but in our minds.

This answering reflex starts in childhood. How do we practice learning to speak? One way is by talking to our parents who deliberately ask us questions so we can learn. "What color is this car?" We respond "the car is red." We also ask questions, an endless number of them from the time we begin to speak, and as our ability to obtain answers increases so does our knowledge. Questions are at the heart of our education process. "Put up your hand if you know the answer!" What is a test but a series of questions that must be answered? Questions also are at the heart of our legal system. It's interesting in this context to recall that you can plead the Fifth Amendment during a trial in order to avoid answering a question, but doing so potentially hurts your credibility. And credibility, as I will highlight in a later chapter, is a critical element of effective communication, both in business and in life.

Every word counts

While questions encourage answers, the answers might not always yield the information you need. The key is to ask quality questions, keeping in mind that every word counts. Changing one word in a question can dramatically change the answer you obtain. Pollsters and survey experts are well aware of this fact. In his book *The Art of Asking Questions* author Stanley L. Payne cites a poll that asked two questions. The questions were identical except for one word.

1. Do you think the United States should allow public speeches against democracy?

2. Do you think the United States should forbid public speeches against democracy?

Since these questions are exact opposites, Payne says that the percentages should be exact opposites (i.e., if 25 percent of the people answered "yes" to the first question then 25 percent should have answered "no" to the second question). However, a much higher percentage of people answered "no" to the second question. The word *forbid*, which is stronger and more negative, prompted a stronger, more negative response.

Every word makes a difference. Take the words *could* and *should* for example.

1. Do you think our company *should* implement a records management program?

2. Do you think our company *could* implement a records management program?

Only one word differs in each question yet they are likely to elicit significantly different answers. The first is more powerful and yields a better chance of motivating a decision maker to consider launching a program. Answering "yes" suggests further questions and discussions around what current challenges are not being met and why it might be prudent to take some immediate actions. The second question is more theoretical, vague and lacks the power to drive further discussion. A decision maker could answer "yes" and easily suggest moving on to another topic.

Quality questions get quality answers

It's up to each of us to formulate good questions that are more likely to obtain the data we want, encourage the actions we want to motivate and gain the results we want to achieve. The foundation of crafting a quality question is to clarify your purpose in asking it. You can define your purpose by – this shouldn't come as a surprise by this point – asking a few concise questions. These include:

1. What do I want to obtain with this question? (information, feedback, an approval, a commitment)

2. Who am I asking? (someone I know well, someone I am not familiar with, a decision maker, an influencer)

3. Is this a good time to ask? (probably not if the question is not critical at the moment and my boss is under a tight deadline to prepare a presentation for the national meeting)

4. Is the question phrased well? (phrased so that I maximize my chance of getting the answer I want)

Let's now look at a hypothetical example of how you might leverage these questions and imagine you are a records manager who wants to drive adoption of a training program.

1. What is my purpose? (Get management to implement a records management training program.)

2. Who am I asking? (Our company's CFO.)

3. When is the right time to ask? (At our monthly department meeting. As head of the department, the CFO attends the meeting and is open to discussing new ideas and programs.)

4. How can I tailor my question? (I know that enterprises in our industry are particularly vulnerable to litigation and that we are not as prepared as we should be for a possible legal discovery request. As part of tailoring my question, I could provide an actual example of what happened to a company that went through a discovery crisis due to lack of training for its records managers.)

Communicating with upper management

All four questions highlighted above underscore an important point. Whether asking questions, listening or exploring answers, when communicating with upper management meet executive needs by clarifying how your proposal will meet the company's overall strategic objectives, rather than one unit or business process.

This approach is particularly important for records and information management professionals when communicating with the organization's leadership. The reason is because upper management has different needs compared with middle management. Senior executives look more for strategic objectives than "how it will be done" details because, after approving a program, they will pass it along to mid-level managers for execution.

This assumes, by the way, that you know your company's strategic objectives. Not all records and information management professionals do. A records management expert once told me that during her presentation at a national conference, she asked records management to write down their company's mission statement. Ninety percent of the seminar participants couldn't articulate their organization's mission statement. Her point: you won't be persuasive with senior executives responsible for funding your initiative if you don't know what the company stands for and where it is going.

The second advantage of questions

Because questions encourage answers, they often yield a second, powerful benefit – they lead to valuable data. The word "question" derives from the word "quest," which is a search for something. In business, the "something" we are most often searching for is information. Why? Because the more valuable our data, the greater our chance of succeeding in our mission. Questions are the critical tool for realizing this success.

In *Bargaining for Advantage*, author G. Richard Schell underscores this point with a statement about what distinguishes skilled negotiators. He asks, "What do skilled negotiators do that average negotiators do not? They ask more than twice the number of questions that average negotiators ask." They ask questions designed to uncover specific information.

In my experience, Schell's point applies to records and information managers as well as virtually every other business function, particularly sales. What do skilled records managers do that average records managers do not? I've observed that, like the best negotiators, they ask at least twice the number of questions. Questions designed to elicit specific data. Questions such as: What cost and time savings can we realize by digitizing our paper records? What are the weaknesses in our disaster recovery program? What steps should we take to improve the security of our records?

Conversely, if you don't ask questions you may be missing critical information. This can invite disastrous business consequences, particularly in journalism. This is precisely what happened several years ago when CBS news correspondent Dan Rather highlighted documents critical of President George W. Bush's National Guard service. Other news sources like *USA Today* and Internet sources asked the important question: have these documents been authenticated by experts? They had not, and Rather's career was basically over.

Dorothy Leeds offers another relevant example:

> "Even journalists, those people we depend on for much of our information, do not ask enough questions. A few years back, NBC was criticized for airing an inaccurate story about the effects of clear-cutting forest in Idaho. The highly regarded network showed two separate scenes of dead fish floating in water, claiming the fish died as an indirect result of the deforestation. It was later discovered that in one of the scenes, the fish weren't even dead. In the other, the stream was not in Idaho.
>
> The mistakes were made because the reporter was unable to attend the editing session, and no one questioned him or his crew to verify the story. In a *New York Times* article, an NBC News staff member said, "It was stupid mistake. It could happen to anybody. But what we learned from this is to question everybody about anything."
>
> (Leeds, 2000)

Be an investigative reporter

Based on the above examples, records and information managers can improve their skills by thinking of themselves as investigative reporters who do ask the right questions at the right time. The foundation of the investigative reporter's approach includes the traditional set of "who, what, when, where and why" questions. If you are a records manager trying to get approval of a project to digitize records for the company's human resources department you might start by asking a few basic, but critical, set of questions:

Who can approve this project?
What are the financial and operational benefits?
When do we anticipate completing the project?
Where do we recommend putting the scanning stations?
Why should we hire a service provider to implement this project?

In preparing your business case you would ask and answer many more questions, but these five can help form the core of your argument and rationalization as to why the project is important and should be approved.

Obstacles to getting information

It would be nice to anticipate that every time we ask quality questions we obtain the valuable information we are seeking. Reality doesn't work this way. The reason has to do with human nature because whether dealing with business colleagues, friends and family or trying to navigate through organizational bureaucracy to get what you need, there are four main obstacles to keep in mind.

The first obstacle is that people don't always volunteer all of the information you might need. They may be too busy, too distracted, too rushed or just not able or willing to pay close attention to your request. For example, you call the box office of a theater to inquire about a show.

"What time does the show start?" you ask.
"It starts at 8 PM."
"When is it over?"
"It's over at 10 PM."
"How much are tickets?"
"They are seventy-five dollars."
"Thanks."

Then you go to the box office to buy tickets and find out that the show was sold out weeks ago. For whatever reason, the box office attendant did not volunteer that critical item of information.

Another obstacle to obtaining valuable information or feedback is that people often answer questions with generalities. You might ask a colleague, for example, "How do you think I performed on that records management project?" Your colleague replies, "I thought you did a great job." If you want more specific, useful feedback you might counter with, "Thanks. Can you tell me what you thought I did particularly well so I can possibly use your feedback on my next project?"

Another example that most of us experience countless times during the day is the word "soon." It's a generality. "I'll get back to you with that information soon." Does that mean you'll respond in five minutes, or in five days? If you want to know you'll have to ask.

A third obstacle to getting the answers we need is that people make assumptions. This is not always the fault of the person speaking to you. Each of us has the responsibility to make sure we understand the information, opinions or feedback we have just been given. It's particularly easy to assume that when discussing a matter with an acknowledged expert, such as a doctor, lawyer or accountant, that they know more than we do. In these situations we may tend not to ask as many questions as we should.

I once consulted a doctor about a pain in my knee. After ordering an MRI that revealed a small cartilage tear, the doctor stated that he could schedule arthroscopic surgery to fix the problem. I could have assumed that this was the only course of action. However, based on experience with the same problem in my other knee I asked the doctor if he thought I could try a few months of physical therapy. If the pain didn't subside, we could schedule the surgery at that point. He agreed. After a few months of physical therapy the pain was gone and I was able to avoid surgery – all because I decided not to make assumptions and instead asked a few important questions.

The fourth obstacle to getting the answers you want is that words and phrases have different meanings to different people. Leeds (2000) cites a perfect example of a beauty pageant where five finalists were all asked the same question, "Can you describe your ideal date?" The judges assumed they were clear in wanting to hear the five women describe their ideal companion. The contestants were in a soundproof booth while one of them answered the question.

Four of the finalists did indeed talk about their ideal man, flowers, candlelight dinners and other romantic scenarios. The fifth finalist, however, stated "My ideal date would be May first because the flowers are starting to bloom and spring is in the air." The words "ideal date" meant something entirely different to her (Leeds, 2000).

It might be helpful in dealing with these four obstacles by thinking of them in reality as one obstacle: making assumptions. If you don't make assumptions, you're less likely to encounter problems based on the fact that someone didn't volunteer all of the critical information you needed. If you don't make assumptions, you often won't settle for generalities but will probe for more useful feedback. If you don't make assumptions, you'll ask for clarification on a word or phrase so that you're less likely to describe a day on the calendar rather than an ideal companion.

The third advantage of questions

Besides encouraging answers and leading to valuable data, questions can also have the advantage of putting you in control. By control I don't mean having power over another person. Rather, it's more about knowing what you want and effectively getting it while considering the rights of others.

One way to consider this concept is by looking at Webster's definition of being aggressive versus being assertive:

Aggressive: a tendency toward unprovoked offenses or invasions.[2]
Assertive: confident and direct in claiming one's rights or putting forward one's views.[3]

I am defining control more in the spirit of achieving a sense of confidence, clarity and directness in expressing your ideas and articulating what you want. You may not obtain the agreement, information or the action you are requesting, but asking questions will give you the kind of control that yields a much better chance of getting your way.

One reason for this is because asking questions enables you to manage your emotional state in a discussion, presentation or situation in which you are trying to resolve a conflict. We're all emotional but it's ineffective to be at the mercy of our emotions, particularly in business.

Out of your right mind

Questions help you get out of a right-brain, sometimes overly emotional state and into a left-brain rational mode of thinking. This is not about squashing your feelings; it's about using questions to balance what you're feeling with the ability to think clearly in the heat of the moment. If you're frustrated with a senior executive who keeps changing his mind about a records management project, for example, instead of flying off the handle you might ask: "Can we make a final decision that will allow us to complete the project on time?" or even better because it's more specific, "What remaining steps will it take for us to reach a final decision so we can complete the project on time?"

Remember that the person who asks the questions controls the direction of the conversation. Ask the right questions and you can steer the conversation in the direction you want it to go. Think of a job interview. If you just sit still and only answer questions, you won't be very impressive or learn much about the company. On the other hand, if you ask questions you're more likely to find out if the job is right for you and to convince the employer that you're right for the job.

One of the ways to clarify this concept about the link between questions and control is to recall your last presentation. Perhaps like many people you were nervous at first but became more comfortable the more you spoke and concentrated on communicating your messages. Then you became nervous again when it became Q&A time. Why? Because you were no longer in control. This is why the President, or any public figure, spends more time preparing for a press conference than for a regular speech. In a press conference the control shifts to members of the press when they start asking challenging and sometimes unanticipated questions.

Ineffective questions

Not all questions, however, are created equal when it comes to gaining control and directing the course of the discussion. Some are effective; some are not. In the latter category are "excuse-provoking" questions. These turn people off and give them an opportunity to provide an excuse. Instead of inquiring, "Why do you keep coming late to our IT staff meetings?" you might instead ask, "This is the third time this month you've been late to our meetings. How can we prevent this from happening again?"

Demeaning questions, which are virtually ineffective 100 percent of the time, are basically using questions as a weapon. They rarely produce a positive answer. "What were you thinking when you came late to the meeting? How could you do such a thing?" These questions simply reinforce negative feelings that may already exist. And because demeaning questions lean much more in the direction of aggression versus assertion, they often generate resentment and fail to solve the problem at hand.

The better approach

The better approach is to ask what I like to refer to as "thought-provoking" questions. These stimulate thought, help people bypass excuses and get into action-oriented thinking. Instead of asking, for example, "Why can't our people access important records fast enough? What's wrong with our program?" you might ask a "What would happen if we …?" question. "What if we brought in an outside consultant to assess our program and suggest ways to improve the speed of accessing records?" That's a question more likely to motivate a positive outcome.

Information-gathering questions are also powerful and effective because they provoke fact-oriented thinking. Instead of asking "Why does it take so long to obtain important human resources data related to our employees?"

you might ask a "What would happen if ...?" question. "What would happen if we scanned our paper-based employee data into an electronic content management system?" The answer just might be quantifiable costs and time savings due to the ability to store and share the records digitally.

The most effective way to gain control of a situation, which is supported by asking effective questions, is to be prepared. Gain as much knowledge as you need ahead of time so that your questions are more likely to get the answers you need. I'll let David Golumb, a past president of the New York Trial Lawyers Association, drive this point home:

> "The most important factor in any situation – whether you're considering buying a car or going to a job interview – is to be prepared. Know as much as possible in advance. Then sit down and think through your questions. What is it that you want to know? If they say X, what are you going to do? If they say Y instead of X, how will that change the situation? That's how I prepare for a witness. I keep refining my questions until I make sure the witness can only give me the answer I want."
>
> (David Golumb cited in Leeds, 2000)

Golumb's advice to "know as much as possible in advance" is critical to the success of any records or IT management initiative. I once had to prepare for a meeting with our company's IT department where each major business unit would discuss initial ideas and requirements for a planned redesign of the corporate intranet. I represented the marketing department; other executives represented finance, human resources, procurement and the IT department itself.

During the three weeks before the meeting was scheduled, I prepared by interviewing a variety of sales and marketing executives, asking questions such as the following:

> How are you using the marketing section of the intranet now?
> When did you last use the section?
> Were you able to find what you were looking for?
> How fast were you able to find it?
> What functionality that the marketing section currently doesn't provide would enable you to do your job better?

I gathered responses to these questions into a brief report along with an analysis of best practices that other companies have shared about how they successfully redesigned their intranets including challenges, solutions, key functionality and the importance of measuring results. The consensus of the meeting was that the marketing department was far ahead of the other business units if defining its requirements had provided valuable input that would help guide the development of the project. Going into the meeting knowing as much as possible in advance about my department's needs and intranet redesign best practices in general made all the difference.

Back to the one-two punch

Another critical advantage of asking quality questions is that it can lead us back to the second effective element of "one-two punch. Asking questions can lead to better listening. Without listening, answers have little value. And most of us believe we are good listeners if for no other reason than we spend a good deal of time engaged in the activity.

As an example, according to listening facts compiled by Laura Janusik, Ph.D., Rockhurst University and made available by the International Listening Association, when it comes to listening and communicating U.S. government managers spend about 13 percent of their time reading, 9 percent writing, 23 percent speaking and a whopping 55 percent listening.[4]

These findings are similar to the general population. Yet despite the relatively substantial amount of time we spend listening, most of us are not very good at it, forgetting most of what we just heard. According to a research study, on average, viewers who just watched and listened to the evening news could only recall 17.2% of the content when not cued, and the cued group never exceeded 25%.[5] Another study found that when presented with a series of unrelated sentences and asked to remember the last word of each sentence, people can only remember, on average, 2.805 items.[6]

Challenges to listening

Why are we such poor listeners? One reason is that most of us receive little, if any, training designed to improve our listening skills.

"Even though most of us spend the majority of our day listening, it is the communication activity that receives the least instruction in school.

Listening training is not required at most universities. Students who are required to take a basic communication course spend less than 7% of class and text time on listening."[7]

Besides lack of training, listening well involves work in the form of focus and concentration. Any life coach, counselor, therapist or successful business person can attest to the fact that listening, far from being a passive activity, is often an arduous task. In addition to the effort it requires, other barriers to listening for business professionals include distractions such as phones ringing and other people talking, personal and internal distractions, such as hunger, headache or preoccupation with something else, and what's referred to as "the rebuttal tendency" – developing a counter argument while the speaker is still speaking.[8]

The rebuttal tendency often leads to one of the biggest challenges to listening, what I refer to as the "Yes, but ..." response. The speaker has finished and the listener, who has not really absorbed and considered the points being made but instead focused on developing the counter argument, is now ready to refute the speaker. The problem with this response is that the listener, who already made up his or her mind while the speaker was talking, never had the opportunity to learn something new. This is why listening is a courageous act. You allow yourself to be vulnerable, open to the possibility of having your viewpoint changed.

What you don't hear can hurt you

Besides missing an opportunity to learning something, not listening can hurt you in other ways. For one, it increases your chances of making mistakes. In my career as a communications professional, I've interviewed many records and IT managers in order to draft articles and case histories designed to promote awareness of a company's technical expertise in these areas. Without listening effectively, I am more apt to get the facts wrong and miss important elements of the story. This puts me in danger of either crafting an inferior article or in the position of having to work harder to write a good piece. These are two scenarios I can avoid by asking good questions and listening effectively in the first place.

Not listening can also lead you down the road of making bad decisions. If you're an IT manager and come out of a meeting where you spend most of the time distracted and not listening attentively, there's a greater chance you could select the wrong software platform for the company's website upgrade. You could have missed some critical details that suggested another platform might be the better choice.

Listening also means being sensitive to your own intuition – in business and life. Each of us has an inner voice that speaks to us and sometimes we suffer when we don't listen to it. That voice often tells us when something is not quite right or it might be prompting us to do something that is right. Remember the records manager who wondered, "What if we are faced with a superfund lawsuit?" Suppose he had ignored the inner prompting that led him to ask that question? His job might have suffered and certainly his company would have suffered.

What you do hear can help you

Let's go down a better road. This one, marked by asking questions and listening carefully, leads to good decisions and many other benefits. One of these benefits is showing people you care, an act that can have a powerful impression on how others perceive you. One of the best examples of this effect I have ever come across is a story related in the book, *Attracting Genuine Love* by Drs. Kathlyn and Gay Hendricks. The story is highlighted in their chapter 10, aptly titled "Listen without interrupting people, including yourself."

> "A friend of ours went to a party where he would be meeting his wife's coworkers from her new job for the first time. He felt anxious as the time for the party grew near, and wondered whether they would like him or not. He rehearsed various scenarios in his mind in which he tried different ways to impress them. He grew more and more tense.
>
> But on the way to the party, the man came up with a radically different approach, one which caused all of his anxiety to melt completely away.
>
> He decided that, instead of trying to impress anyone, he would spend the evening simply listening to them and summarizing what they had just said. At the party, he spent the evening listening carefully to everyone, responding with phrases like, 'I understand what you're saying, you feel strongly that . . .' and 'Let me see if I understand what you mean . . .' He also avoided voicing his own opinions, even though at times it meant biting his tongue to keep from doing so.
>
> To his amazement, he discovered that no one noticed or remarked on the fact that he was just listening. Each person he talked to during the evening seemed content to be listened to without interruption. On the

way home, his wife (whom he had not told about the experiment) told him that a number of people had made a point of telling her what a remarkable person he was. The word 'charismatic' was used by one person to describe him, while another said he was one of the most 'articulate' people she had ever met.

Could it be that charisma and brilliance have as much to do with how we listen as what we say? Imagine a world where people actually listen to one another, rather than just waiting for the other people to stop talking so they can give their opinion."

(Hendricks and Hendricks, 2004)

The persuasion factor

Besides generating a positive impression, listening intently can sometimes enable you to take a more subtle, insightful approach in encouraging another person to agree with your point of view. This is a method of persuasion by getting people to persuade themselves. Listening carefully, you can craft questions that might prompt a senior executive to convince herself that your proposed program is the right solution for the company.

This approach can also encourage a sales prospect, for example, to think about the reasons he might want to purchase your product or service. Leeds (2000) relates a story in which a director in a brokerage firm asked her to design a training program for his firm. She did and he told her to come in to sign the agreement. She arrived at his office and he said he was no longer interested. She was devastated but instead of trying to convince him he was wrong she listened closely to his reasons and then asked a key question: "You were so interested when we first spoke. What was it that made you so excited about it two weeks ago?"

He started to talk, got all excited about the program again and in five minutes said, "Let's do it." He signed the agreement. The persuasive force to do so came from him, not her. That's the secret. *People believe what they say, not what you say.*

Give them psychological air

Simply listening before asking a well-placed question gives people some space in which to consider, in their own words, why they should adopt your solution. The importance of that pause, that "space," is a critical component of getting what you want. Author Stephen Covey in his bestselling *The 7 Habits of Highly Effective People* describes this as giving the other person "psychological air." It's not only a persuasive act, but also deeply therapeutic and healing.

> "If all the air were suddenly sucked out of the room you're in right now, what would happen to your interest in this book? You wouldn't care about the book; you wouldn't care about anything except getting air. Survival would be your only motivation.
>
> But now that you have air, it doesn't motivate you. This is one of the greatest insights in the field of human motivation: *Satisfied needs do not motivate*. It's only the unsatisfied need that motivates. Next to physical survival, the greatest need of a human being is psychological survival – to be understood, to be affirmed, to be validated, to be appreciated.
>
> When you listen with empathy to another person, you give that person psychological air. And after that vital need is met, you can then focus on influencing or problem solving.
>
> This need for psychological air impacts communication in every area of life."
>
> (Covey, 1989)

Keys to better listening

One way to approach improving your listening skills is to know what to listen for. This includes listening *for feeling*, which can yield insight into the true intent of the speaker. Listening for feeling is listening between the lines or listening with the heart. It's more right-brain listening. When we speak we use vocal variety to help make ourselves understood. We emphasize certain words and phrases over others. When you are listening, it's important to pay attention to nuances such as stress placed on certain words and the emotion of the voice. Consider, for example, the differences in the following hypothetical responses to a proposal you just presented:

- I don't think, at this point, we would be interested in launching a records management program. (I haven't convinced one executive.)

- I don't think, *at this point*, we would be interested in launching a records management program. (Now may not be the right time. Perhaps later in the year.)

- I don't think, at this point, *we* would be interested in launching a records management program. (Maybe not this group of executives, but perhaps other executives or departments in the company might be interested in and benefit from the program.)

You can also listen *for content*, or facts. This is listening with the left side of the brain; making sure you understand what is being said; you have the information you need; and that you're not making false assumptions.

One way to improve your skill at listening for facts is to listen as if you will have to explain what is being said to someone else. For example, an executive has just made an important point about a proposed records management program. You could say, "Let me be sure I have this right. You are saying that updating our records retention policy is a good idea, but you're not sure everyone on the team will agree?" Rephrase the executive's comment to make sure you're on the same wavelength.

Another way to become adept at listening for facts is to judge the content of what someone is saying, not the way they are saying it. People may not use the right words in your opinion, or say things in a manner you would prefer, but that that does not mean you should discount what they're saying. In my experience this is a very valuable practice because in business, as in life, not all talented and insightful people have an effective or even pleasant communication style. If you can listen beyond their style, however, you could potentially gain valuable information that helps in getting what you want.

A third key to better listening is to listen for *who is speaking*. This is making ourselves aware of the credentials of the person with whom we are interacting. We tend to listen more carefully to people we think are important. However, it is easy to appear authoritative; that does not necessarily make it so. Part of quality listening is to determine who is worth listening to. Would you listen seriously to what someone, who has no background in accounting, is telling you to do about refinancing a second mortgage on your home?

When you listen for who is speaking, try asking yourself the questions highlighted in Table 3.1.

Taking it to a whole new level

Being receptive – asking effective questions and really listening – provides the one-two punch that can significantly further your communication skills

Table 3.1 Listening for who is speaking

Question	Issue
Is this person qualified to speak on this subject?	As a records manager, when it comes to compliance or risk management issues, you want to deal with someone who knows what they're doing
What underlying motives might this person have?	If you go to a surgeon for a medical opinion, he's likely to recommend surgery
Does this person have any prejudices or beliefs that will compromise his objectivity?	If you talk to your doctor about nutrition, he or she may have a belief that taking vitamins is a waste of time

and help ensure success in your records or IT management career. Asking questions can uncover the important information you need to take the right action, put you in control and enable you to listen better. Listening more effectively enables you to be perceived positively and to be more persuasive in gaining what you want.

Being brief, clear and receptive, however, can only take you so far if you don't know what you're trying to achieve. Being aware of your purpose, and consistently keeping it in mind, can bring your communications effectiveness to a whole new level. This is the core of the next chapter, in which I'll spotlight the power of being strategic.

Notes

1. Leeds provides a comprehensive look at how questions are an essential tool of the seeker and the problem-solver in our personal and professional lives.
2. Retrieved 3 June 2013 from *http://dictionary.reference.com/browse/aggressive?s=t*
3. Retrieved 3 June 2013 from *http://dictionary.reference.com/browse/assertive?s=t&ld=1134*
4. International Listening Association, "Listening facts." Retrieved 15 July 2013 from *http://d1025403.site.myhosting.com/files.listen.org/Facts.htm*
5. International Listening Association, "Listening and memory."

Retrieved 15 July 2013 from *http://d1025403.site.myhosting.com/files.listen.org/Facts.htm # Memory*

6. International Listening Association, "Listening and memory." Retrieved 15 July 2013 from *http://d1025403.site.myhosting.com/files.listen.org/Facts.htm # Memory*

7. International Listening Association, "Listening and education." Retrieved 15 July 2013 from *http://d1025403.site.myhosting.com/files.listen.org/Facts.htm # Barriers*

8. International Listening Association, "Listening barriers." Retrieved 15 July 2013 from *http://d1025403.site.myhosting.com/files.listen.org/Facts.htm # Barriers*

4

Be strategic: what am I trying to achieve?

"In preparing for battle I've always found that plans are useless, but planning is essential."

(Dwight Eisenhower)

Abstract: Strategic communication is communication with clear purpose in mind. To be effective, strategic communication ideally targets a problem and a creative solution to that problem backed by a plan and a network of relationships that can help you complete your goal. Another key to fulfilling your purpose is to know the difference between strategic and expressive communication and use them accordingly. Strategic communication is about influencing others. Expressive communication is about expressing thoughts and feelings. While important, expressive communication most often will not give you the best chance for motivating others. Another foundation of strategic communication is to be aware of your own communication style. Generally, communication styles fall into two categories: self-oriented and other-oriented.

Key words: strategic communication, expressive communication, purposeful, relationship network, credibility, influence, persuasiveness, communication style, core beliefs, enthusiasm, conviction, tailoring the message.

Perhaps the most effective way to accomplish a mission, in business and in life, is to know your purpose, have a thorough plan to fulfill that purpose and to take effective steps in carrying out your plan. Strategic communication is similar. It's communication backed by a purpose and a plan. Your purpose comes first, and being clear about it is critical to communicating with maximum influence and persuasion. I compare it with fixing your eye on the target, whether the target is a bull's-eye, the finish line, a job offer or a sales contract.

The principle of creating things twice

Author Stephen Covey offers excellent insights about how to understand and leverage the power of purpose. These insights include the principle that all things are created twice (Covey, 1989). The mental creation comes first, then the physical creation. If you're going to launch a records management program, for example, you think about every detail that the program should encompass. You have a clear idea of the kind of program you want to implement. The potential elements of the program might be numerous and include an initial assessment of the company's recordkeeping processes, creation of recordkeeping policies and procedures and provisions for communicating them to employees and periodically updating them, guidelines for retaining and disposing records as well as countless other details. You incorporate these elements into a blueprint, develop the blueprint into a plan and then marshal the physical resources you need to implement the plan. The key is to begin this entire process, as Covey puts it, "with the end in mind."

Keeping the end in mind

What does it mean to "begin with the end in mind?" It means having a clear understanding of your goal. It means knowing your destination so that you can continually monitor the steps you are taking and continually adjust to ensure that you are going in the right direction. Here's how Covey describes the process:

> "If you want to have a successful enterprise, you clearly define what you're trying to accomplish. You carefully think through the product or service you want to provide in terms of your market target, then you organize all the elements – financial, research and development, operations, marketing, personnel, physical facilities, and so on – to meet that objective. The extent to which you begin with the end in mind often determines whether or not you are able to create a successful enterprise. Most business failures begin in the first creation, with problems such as undercapitalization, misunderstanding of the market, or lack of a business plan."
>
> (Covey, 1989)

To different degrees, we use the principles of the two creations and beginning with the end in mind in many areas of our lives. We determine our destination and plan the best route before we go on a trip. We detail presentations before we give them and carefully craft the elements of a program before we propose it. In addition to these principles I would suggest adding a third: strategic communication. Once we have our eye on the target, using strategic communication can be a vital tool for enabling us to hit the bulls-eye.

Strategic versus expressive communication

There are two broad categories of communication for human beings and understanding the difference between them is critical for achieving business success. The purpose of strategic communication is to motivate and influence someone to take action, whether to go on a date with you or accept your business proposal. However, if you are going to influence someone, you need to take the time to understand them and tailor your message to them. This means your communication is purposeful; not just about you but as much about the other person. This form of communication offers the best chance of helping you get what you want in business.

Expressive communication, the other major form of interacting with others, is different. It is not designed to motivate others. It is about expressing thoughts and feelings. It's about "me." I don't necessarily need you to do anything. I just need you to listen. No doubt this type of contact is important, but it will not give you that "best chance" of motivating others in business.

Avoid being a "yelling coach"

On the contrary, many people make the critical mistake of using expressive communication to motivate others. It rarely works and sometimes has the opposite effect to what we intend. A great example of this is the story of "the yelling coach," highlighted in *Power Talk: The Art of Effective Communication* by Howard J. Rankin, Ph.D.

"Many years ago I was part of a team of psychologists researching social interaction between the staff and players of a leading professional soccer team. It was the habit of one of the coaches to sit on the bench yelling profane criticism at the players in an effort to motivate them. When the data were analyzed it was found that the main effect of these supposedly motivational tirades was that all the players avoided that part of the field that was in earshot of the coach!"

(Rankin, 1999)[1]

Rankin goes on to point out that while expressing feelings can help relieve pent-up tension and provide many other forms of therapeutic value, it is self-centered communication that does not require consideration of anyone else. That's precisely why it doesn't work well in business. It doesn't motivate anyone to buy products, accept proposals or improve performance.

The biggest communication mistake

In my experience the biggest communication mistake most people make in business is that they use expressive, self-centered communication when they are trying to motivate and influence others. This approach often leads, as it did with the yelling coach, to miscommunication, frustration and failure. One reason for this is that many of us are unclear about the exact purpose of our communication. We are not sure about what we are trying to achieve and consequently are not using the right tools to reach our goals – goals that we have not articulated.

Another reason this strategy doesn't work is that using expressive communication to motivate is often accompanied by "magical thinking." Behind magical thinking is the belief that influence is possible simply because I strongly wish it to be so. I convince myself that if I yell loud enough, my players will be motivated to play better and win. I choose to believe that if I criticize a staff member in front of others during a meeting, he or she will improve.

These expressions of feelings and thoughts, however, rarely influence others to act in ways we would like. Instead, as in the yelling coach story, people move away so they don't hear the high-pitched insults. Or, a staff member may bear criticism with silent resentment and eventually find another job.

A third reason many people use expressive communication inappropriately is that many of us have never been trained in purposeful communication. How many courses or seminars have you taken in communicating strategically, improving your listening skills or advancing your ability to influence others? If you have taken the time to train in these areas, you are ahead of most of the general population.

The key point to remember is that expressive communication is natural because it is the way we start communicating from birth. Using it is instinctive. Strategic communication is more challenging. It requires training and more effort to use effectively because we have to tailor our messages to the needs of the audience. Without meeting these challenges, we most likely will continue to use expressive communication in situations where strategic communication would be a better choice.

The relationship factor

To communicate in a way that maximizes your chances of getting what you want, there are other challenges to overcome besides mistakenly using a self-centered approach to motivate others. One challenge involves understanding that all persuasion at work begins within a network of relationships. If those relationships are weak, you may have a huge barrier to break through in order to get your idea across or get your proposal approved. G. Richard Shell and Mario Moussa, Directors of the Wharton School's Strategic Persuasion Workshop, underscore the importance of relationships.

> "A relationship with someone, somewhere, will be the starting point for putting your idea in 'play,' and relationships with and between people you may not even know will often be the end point for getting it adopted. You need a circle of influence, a network of people who know people who know people. And it may be too late to form such a circle when you are ready to make your sale. The relationships must already be in place. The biggest barriers, of course, arise when you face negative or hostile relationships in the pathway of your idea."

> (Shell and Moussa, 2008)[2]

The credibility factor

Another barrier concerns credibility, which is one of the most critical factors of all when it comes to communicating strategically and – the subject of Chapter 5 – persuasively. One of the best definitions of credibility I've ever come across is a quote by author Clarence B. Randall: "The leader must know; must know that he knows; and must make it abundantly clear to others that he knows" (Randall, 1964). This to me is the essence of credibility. It's about perceived competence. People will not have confidence in you unless they believe you know what you're talking about.

Think about the job interview process. One of the keys to securing a job offer is to convince everyone you speak with that you know your stuff and can translate that in-depth knowledge into decisions and actions that will benefit the organization. For this reason many executive recruiters advise that, to whatever extent possible, you should start "doing the job" in the interview. This means coming prepared with as much knowledge about the organization as possible and being ready to offer ideas about potential programs and strategies that can promote the company's success. This is a way of demonstrating that "I am credible. I have the talent, experience and abilities that you're looking for."

An important part of credibility is character, which includes qualities such as honesty, courage and integrity. In fact Aristotle argued that character was the most important persuasion tool of them all.[3] Therefore maintaining and continuously improving your character is essential to success not only in communication, but business in general. Banking tycoon J.P. Morgan summed up this idea in a short exchange he had with a congressional committee in the early 1900s:

Committee member   Is not commercial credit based primarily on money or property?

J.P. Morgan   No, sir. The first thing is character.

Committee member   Before money or property?

J.P. Morgan   Before money or anything else. Money cannot buy it.

(Shell and Moussa, 2008)

The connection factor

Besides weak relationships and lack of credibility, another challenge to effective, strategic, purposeful communication is failure to establish a meaningful connection with your audience. Whether an auditorium filled with hundreds of people, a small group of senior executives or a single colleague sitting across the table from you at lunch, you're far more likely to get your way if you create a strong rapport with others. A good way to accomplish this goal is to discover and share what you have in common with your audience, particularly similar experiences. Here's the way author Howard Rankin emphasizes this important point:

"Knowing that an experience has been shared by another human being is a very powerful force. In many ways, human beings live alone in their own minds and they are always looking for ways to share their experiences. Shared experiences are validated experiences. The thought that another human being has shared similar experiences is empowering precisely because it addresses the fundamental need to feel that we are not alone. Similarity is therefore an essential component of communication. One of the first tasks of a communicator it to establish symmetry with his or her listener. There are many possible points of similarity."

(Rankin, 1999)

One of the "many possible points of similarity" Rankin refers to is establishing how your goals are compatible with those of the listener. If you can make the case that your goals are actually the same, so much the better. For example, senior management may not be inclined to incur the costs of assessing and potentially improving the organization's current records management program. Both management and the recordkeeping department, however, share the mutual goals of minimizing risk and enhancing compliance while ensuring that employees have timely access to records. Promoting awareness of how an improved program can better help the organization meet these shared goals will go a long way toward winning approval to take action.

How can you discover what goals you have in common with your listener? If you guessed that the answers come from the previous chapter – ask the right questions and listen carefully – you are on target. This approach gives you the ability to define the listener's goals in their own terms while demonstrating how they are similar to your own. Then you can detail how you are going help both sides realize these goals, including the strategies and actions you will put into play to get the job done.

The core beliefs factor

There's one approach almost guaranteed to invite rejection. Ask your audience to buy into any of your ideas or proposals that violate their basic values or beliefs, particularly if those standards have been articulated in procedures, policies and other written formats. For example, your company might be conservative when it comes to risk. Proposing a new, high-risk product or service, no matter what the potential gains, is an idea that probably will not fly.

Why is this mistake such an idea killer? The reason is it puts people in an uncomfortable bind. Either they go with your idea and sacrifice their core belief, or they go with their belief and reject your idea. People will usually do the latter because core beliefs are very strong, representing a commitment that has often existed for many years to the point of being largely unconscious.

Years ago I watched an interview with author Deepak Chopra, in which he cited a study that illustrated the power of unconscious commitment. Researchers inserted a glass panel into a fish bowl that essentially cut the area of the bowl in half. For a time, the fish continually bumped up against the glass panel. After a period of time, the researchers removed the glass panel. The fish continued to stay in one side of the bowl, never crossing the border where the glass panel had been inserted. Chopra pointed out that the experiment offers a powerful analogy to human belief systems. We can become committed to believing things that are no longer true, or perhaps have never been true, and these beliefs can become unconscious. They become thoughts that we no longer question.

Conscious beliefs can be just as powerful, which is why it makes sense to position our ideas in a way that is consistent with our audience's beliefs. A true story about how a store manager, Bob Bogle, persuaded Sam Walton to name his first large discount store Wal-Mart (later to become Walmart). Walton did not like to parade his ego. Bogle decided, therefore, instead of going against Walton's resistance to self-promotion, he would appeal to one of Walton's core beliefs: saving money. Here is Bogle's account, as related in Walton's autobiography, *Made in America*:

> "I scribbled W-A-L-M-A-R-T on the bottom of [a] card, and said [to Sam] 'To begin with there's not as many letters to buy.' I had bought the letters that said 'Ben Franklin,' and I knew how much it cost to put them up and to light them and repair the neon, so I said 'This is just seven letters.' He didn't say anything, and I dropped the subject. A few days

later I went by to see when we could start setting the fixtures in the building, and I saw that our sign maker ... already had the W-A-L up there and was headed up the ladder with an M. ... I just smiled and went on."

(Shell and Moussa, 2008)

Bogle was successful because he avoided going against one of Walton's core beliefs – "I shouldn't parade my ego" – and instead appealed to his firm belief in the value of low cost.

The personal needs factor

A fifth challenge to heed in successful strategic communication is the importance of focusing on your audience's interests, wants and needs. Help meet their needs and your ability to influence increases substantially. I'll address this concept in greater detail in Chapter 6. For now I'll spotlight two examples. One is a need that we all have: the need to feel like a winner whether in sports, business, personal relationships or any important area of our lives.

One relatively simple way to help someone feel like a winner is to give them more than they expect. For instance, if you're a business owner with a customer who has given you a lot of consistent business, give that customer a discount without waiting for them to ask.

When I was a young boy I witnessed my father embodying this idea of making others feel like winners. One day I accompanied him to our local dry cleaner to pick up some items. At the front counter, my father asked the owner if his presser was working in the back. The owner said he was and suddenly I noticed my father heading for the back. Little did I know that for some time my father had been impressed with the quality of the presser's work. Suits, pants, shirts and everything else the presser touched came back as if they were brand new. I remember seeing my father say a few words to the presser, shake his hand and give him a generous tip. The look on the presser's face was priceless. It was the look of a winner.

The other example concerns the ability to appeal to what others want. A story about Andrew Carnegie perfectly sums up this skill. Carnegie had two nephews attending college. The boys' parents were dismayed that no matter what they tried, they couldn't motivate their sons to write home. Carnegie bet one hundred dollars that without spending a penny or exercising any special form of intimidation he could succeed. The parents gave him the go-ahead, doubting that he could do it. Carnegie then wrote the boys a letter saying that he enclosed some money for each of them. However, he didn't enclose any money.

The nephews immediately wrote home asking if their uncle had forgotten to add something when mailing the letter. Carnegie won the bet because he understood the power of appealing to others' self-interest (Shell and Moussa, 2008).

This strategy can also work even when people aren't clear about what they want – a situation that provides an opportunity to educate people about their own interests and needs. You may not be aware of the extent to which security is important to your enterprise. But if I demonstrate how effective recordkeeping can protect your company against risks such as a legal discovery demand, you may decide that such protection is in your self-interest. Therefore, it would be worthwhile to engage my services to create and launch a program.

Meeting the challenge

The best way to begin to meet these strategic communication challenges is to heed the ancient Greek aphorism that was inscribed in the forecourt of the temple of Apollo at Delphi: "know thyself." Purposeful communication starts with being aware of your own communication style. Without this self-awareness, you won't have the ability to adapt your style to others. This means your purposeful communication skills will be limited at best or extremely poor due to constant critical communication mismatches at worst. Remember that the essence of strategic communication is being able to tailor your message to your audience. For a prime example of how to practice this art – of how to get outside of your frame of reference and into others' – let's look at one of the most skillful communicators in American history, Abraham Lincoln.

Strategic communication par excellence

In her book *Team of Rivals*, Doris Kearns Goodwin tells the story of how Lincoln faced a major challenge after he won the 1860 election: getting William H. Seward to join his cabinet. Seward had been the Republican favorite going into the party's convention. He misjudged Lincoln's political skill and lost. Lincoln knew that Seward would not only be an asset to the country's leadership, it would help Lincoln consolidate his Republican base. However, Seward and his supporters were reeling from the defeat.

Their pride was hurt and the last thing they had on their mind was doing what was right for the country. Lincoln set out to use his communications skills to win Seward over.

Lincoln's first step was to step outside his own frame of reference and see things from Seward's point of view. This meant acknowledging Seward's need to maintain status despite the defeat. Lincoln decided to offer Seward the most sought-after post in the cabinet, secretary of state. Lincoln also considered Seward's reputation by forwarding the offer through his vice president rather than making it public and subject to speculation in the press. Additionally, Lincoln addressed Seward's injured ego by drafting two letters for the vice president to carry to Seward.

The first letter expressed the formal offer for the secretary of state position. The second letter, marked confidential, was equally important. It was meant to deal with the possibility that Seward would be offended by the offer, thinking it was a tactic to placate him and his supporters. Seward reportedly was agitated when he opened the first letter containing the formal offer. Then he opened the second letter, which stated:

> "Rumors have got into the newspapers to the effect that the Department, named above, would be tendered to you as a compliment, and with the expectation that you would decline it. I beg you to be assured that I have said nothing to justify these rumors. On the contrary, it has been my purpose, from the day of the nomination in Chicago, to assign you, by your leave, this place in the administration . . . I now offer you the place, in the hope that you will accept it, and with the belief that your position in the public eye, your integrity, ability, learning, and great experience, all combine to render it an appointment pre-eminently fit to be made."

What a difference the second letter made. According to the vice president's account of the meeting, Seward's face became "pale with excitement" and after reading the letter he enthusiastically shook the vice president's hand. Seward accepted the job and helped Lincoln recruit the rest of the cabinet. In fact, Seward became such a close and trusted part of Lincoln's team that he was also targeted for assassination by members of John Wilkes Booth conspiracy on 14 April 1865.[4]

A question of style

Lincoln was successful in recruiting Seward because he took the time to consider what was important to Seward. He was able to step outside of his own ego and assess the situation from another person's point of view.

To do this, you need to be aware that most communication approaches fall into two categories, other-oriented and self-oriented. The former approach, embodied by how Lincoln dealt with Seward, is marked by tailoring the message and a careful consideration of the other's viewpoint. The latter is a blunt announcement delivered to whoever is listening. Consideration of how others might react is usually minimal. These two approaches are usually backed by one of three styles: high key, moderate or low key.

Business professionals tend to favor, consciously or unconsciously, one approach and one style in their communication. That is not to say they won't occasionally mix approaches and styles, but most often they will stay in their comfort zone. An example of one approach and style will help you become more aware of the manner in which you usually communicate.

Grove swings the bat

Let's look at someone who embodied the self-oriented, aggressive style described in the often-used phrase, "Do this my way or hit the highway." CEO Andy Grove was well known for his tough, pile-driving method of communication. One Intel executive, Scott Gibson, recalled the day Grove opened a meeting to which a few executives slipped in a bit late. Grove kept a wooden bat near his chair. When the latecomers took the seats Grove fell silent, and then slammed the bat on the table exclaiming in a shout that he didn't ever want to be in a meeting with the group that didn't start and end when it was scheduled. Intel became famous for on-time meetings.

Grove's approach was self-oriented and high key. However, and most importantly, Grove was aware of his style and he didn't want it to hurt innovation at Intel and he also wanted to avoid going down in business history as a petty tyrant. As a result, he fostered a culture at Intel that allowed others to be high key and fight for good ideas that they felt passionate about. Grove described this cultural norm as "constructive confrontation." Other executives had license to be as direct as Grove. Confrontations weren't personal, they were business.

A good example of the Intel culture in action concerned Grove's assistant, Sue McFarland, who Grove decimated in a job review saying she had no ambition and didn't deserve a raise. McFarland left the office in tears. She went home, regained her composure and remembered that constructive confrontation was a two-way street. After composing a detailed business case that refuted each of Grove's charges she went back and confronted him. She walked out of the office with a raise and permission to hire an assistant (Jackson, 1998; Shell and Moussa, 2008).

Other executives who might be described as owning a similar self-oriented, high-key style include Donald Trump and Bill Gates. Trump once stated about himself: "I can be a screamer when I want to be" (Trump, 1987). One real estate executive for whom I implemented public relations and marketing programs confirmed this about Trump. Having worked with Trump on several deals, the executive stated that if you agreed to provide Trump something by 9 AM on Monday, by 9:01 AM on Monday Trump was on the phone to confirm you had met the terms. If not, you got yelled at. As for Gates, he was described by one of his Harvard professors in this way: "He's an obnoxious human being ... He'd put people down when it was not necessary, and just generally was not a pleasant fellow to have around the place" (Manes and Andrews, 1983).

Rockefeller calls their bluff

For contrast, it's helpful to see how an opposite, other-oriented approach and low-key style can be just as effective in using strategic communication to meet a business objective. Like Andy Grove, the example involves an icon in American industry, John D. Rockefeller. Known to be a quiet, calculating businessman, at one point early in his career Rockefeller was trapped in a partnership with three older men, two of which, James and Richard Clark, tried continually to take advantage of Rockefeller's youth by treating him more like an underling than a partner.

The third partner, Samuel Andrews, was Rockefeller's ally and they both wanted to invest heavily in the oil business. However, the Clark brothers continually vetoed Rockefeller's ideas, treating him with arrogance and condescension. Rockefeller wanted out of the partnership but there was a major legal obstacle: the partnership could only be dissolved if all members of the firm agreed to it. The Clark brothers threatened to pull out, but they were only bluffing. Rockefeller knew this and quietly plotted his moves.

First, behind the scenes Rockefeller lined up support from several banks and his ally, Samuel Andrews. Then he provoked another quarrel with the Clark brothers, during which they uttered the words Rockefeller wanted to hear about threatening to pull out of the firm and leave Rockefeller to his own devices.

Rockefeller set up another meeting with all of the partners at his home later in the day. His strategy was playing out perfectly. The Clarks came to the meeting with the goal of intimidating Rockefeller into submission. They threatened to dissolve the company. Rockefeller and Samuel Andrews agreed. The Clarks left the meeting believing they had won and that Rockefeller would fall in line.

Nothing could be further from the truth. Rockefeller immediately went to the local newspaper and placed a formal notice that he and his partners had unanimously agreed to part ways. The Clarks, trapped by their own bluff, read in the next day's newspaper that they were out of business. The Clarks called a meeting with Rockefeller who confirmed that he indeed wanted to break up. Rockefeller paid them off and in three years, at the age of 28, became head of the largest oil refiner in the world and went on to become one of the richest men in American history (Chernow, 1998; Shell and Moussa, 2008).

While it might be easy to view Rockefeller's tactics as manipulative, it's important to remember that he was continually being ignored and bullied. His response was to communicate in a more moderate tone and use an other-oriented approach by playing to the Clark brothers' interests. Strategically he arranged the situation so that the resolution actually came from the Clark brothers themselves. By threatening yet again to leave the partnership, they gave Rockefeller what he wanted. Like Lincoln with Seward – although in this case the goal was much different – Rockefeller demonstrated he was a perceptive judge of human character and able to assume the viewpoint of others in crafting his strategy. Again, this is the essence of taking a strategic approach.

It begins with solutions

Once you're aware of your communications approach and style, you're ready to begin communicating strategically. It all starts with proposing solutions and the key to proposing solutions is to clearly define the problem you are trying to solve. The more accurately you can define a problem, the better. With a well-defined problem you're more apt to craft a solution that has a good chance of working. Then the next step is to decide who you need to influence or team with in order to get the solution implemented. Let's look at a case history example that illustrates this process of defining the problem, targeting the solution and getting the right players on board to make it happen.

Lack of accountability

This case spotlights problems caused by lack of accountability for the records management function and how creating accountability was the solution that helped solve those problems. The company involved is a commercial builder and general contracting firm with billions in annual revenue and over a thousand employees. The firm worked with an outside service provider that managed a range of mail, print and document-scanning activities as well as directed management of hard-copy records and storage of records in a warehouse.

The builder initially faced a number of records management challenges due to its decentralized culture and lack of corporate accountability for records management. In particular, the company was incurring over $1 million in legal settlement costs annually that involved subcontractors because the builder could not locate records that would prove its case. Once a construction project was finished, records were stored anywhere there was room, including construction yards and construction trailers parked in fields waiting development. Additionally, historic documents were not being preserved.

One of the firm's executives saw the situation clearly and defined the problem. The lack of accountability for storing and preserving records was costing the firm significant money. Things started to change when the executive marshaled the support of several colleagues. The team assessed the situation, clarified the problem and then proposed the solution to senior management. The solution was to manage records at the corporate level since that is where the liability exists.

A creative solution

The proposal included a creative move – assigning the vice president of property management to assume responsibility for the records program. One reason she was assigned was that she already had relationships with the firm's construction managers. The other reason was more subtle and interesting. She was assigned the responsibility not because she had in-depth expertise in records management, but because she was already working with the builder's outside service provider, which did have the records expertise and was already engaged in some records management activities. The outside firm was excited to be given the opportunity to work with the Vice President because it demonstrated that the organization was taking its records management issues seriously.

With all the pieces in place it was time to implement several important fixes. The service provider, working as both consultant and project leader on the initiative, arranged for records that had historic value to be sent to a records warehouse adjacent to the corporate headquarters and for all records to be better managed. The latter included creating a records retention schedule. The previous schedule wasn't researched, focused only on legal requirements and did not take business requirements into consideration. Also, no one was accountable for the schedule. The Vice President in charge knew she had to take ownership of getting a revised retention schedule and assumed responsibility to champion the service provider's implementing it as a critical part of the program.

Executive-level buy-in

It's easy to state the importance of having a retention policy, schedule and procedures supported by training, auditing and reporting. However, if the policy doesn't have executive-level sponsorship, all of these efforts are likely to fall short. The service provider was good at networking, a critical element of strategic communication. The provider successfully launched the new records program activities because it leveraged the fact that high-level personnel were involved and these individuals were holding each other accountable. For instance, all documentation was drafted and presented to the vice president for edits and buy-in. She then presented the documents to the management committee in order to get the retention schedule and disposition program implemented.

Accountability was supported in other ways. The service provider installed records management software to track the movement of records, to manage legal and audit holds and to help decide disposition (i.e., whether a document should be destroyed or uploaded into the company's archive system for preservation). Open communication of all information was made available on the company's intranet, which included records management program information, forms, policies, procedures and training information and which further held the employees accountable for understanding their roles and responsibilities.

Tangible business benefits

The situation was turned around because an executive saw the problem, gathered a supporting team, obtained senior management support and ultimately helped the builder implement a creative solution. The service provider was able to launch new approaches because it had the right executive-level champion involved and a committee to ensure buy-in from various departments. Now there is full accountability for a well-defined program that allows the company to legally defend itself if necessary. Also, the employees have full understanding of their responsibilities.

This is a case where taking a strategic approach yielded solutions that drove tangible business benefits, some of which included:

- Annual net litigation costs were reduced from $1 million to $50,000.

- Legal hold notices were communicated and disposition suspended through the centralized software.

- The vice president continued to be the point person for communication.

- Records management became one of the builder's most valuable assets.

Work your network

You may have noticed in the case history that the executive's initial vision would probably have never become a reality without gathering the support of the right people. Securing such support before you propose your solution and begin implementing it is often a critical component of success. Notice that I emphasize not only obtaining support, but support of the "right people." The people you need to make your idea happen may be different at each stage of solution development, from selling the idea to implementing it, monitoring results and, if appropriate, continuously improving it. The most effective approach is not only getting to know the right people (if you don't already) and obtaining their support. It includes rewarding them for their support in whatever way makes sense, even it's just a simple acknowledgement of the importance of their contribution, and also making sure they're aware your support is available when they need it.

A lesson from Mandela

I want to drive home the importance of forging relationships with the right people by citing an example that is far from the corporate boardroom. This example comes from a jail cell. Nelson Mandela was incarcerated in the brutal Robben Island prison for over 26 years. One of the ways he survived was by having a goal, to improve the treatment of his fellow prisoners in any way he could. Next, he developed relationships with the right people. These were not the prison's highest officials; they were the lowest level employees, the warders. Mandela's insight was that in order to carry out his mission, he needed cooperation from the workers who actually had the most control over the prisoner's lives, and these individuals were the warders. As Mandela found out:

"The most important person in any prisoner's life is not the minister of justice, not the commissioner of prisons, not even the head of the prison, but the warder in one's section. If you needed an extra blanket, and went to the minister of justice, you would get no response. If you went to the commissioner of prisons, the commissioner would say, 'It's against regulations.' If you went to the head of the prison, he would respond, 'If I give you an extra blanket, I must give one to everyone.' But if you were on good terms with the warder, the warder would simply go to the stockroom and fetch a blanket. In addition, and perhaps most important, when you had a good relationship with the warders, it became difficult for the higher-ups to treat you roughly."

(Mandela, 1994)

Mandela provides a powerful example of a person who has a strategic vision – improving prison conditions – and developing relationships with the people who could help realize that vision in many ways such as securing extra blankets for those who needed them.

It's no different in the business world, where different stakeholders can make unique contributions toward helping you meet your strategic objective. The size of the team you'll need to marshal will vary at different stages of the game. Shell and Moussa offer some useful guidelines to keep in mind:

"Research shows that an average of twenty people inside an organization are involved in the approval of most important new ideas. And each of those twenty people will likely have some effect on the final outcome. Even relatively simple ideas require input and approval from an average of eight people. Thus, although someone in a high position may eventually be called upon to make the 'go–no go' decision on a new idea, it is rare that authority alone dictates the shape, size, and scope of a new initiative."

(Shell and Moussa, 2008)

Six months and 18 people

I recently worked on a website redesign project that underscores how a team of people is often needed to keep an idea on a successful path from inception through implementation and completion. A chief marketing officer for a technology company pinpointed problems with the organization's website. Graphics were outdated, the site's navigation wasn't optimal and important content was missing. The executive researched these and other challenges, worked with an outside web design firm to target solutions and then consolidated support from the firm's senior leadership team. That totaled six people so far.

With the project approved, another team of "the right people" was brought on board to complete the changes within a deadline of approximately six months. The team included five people from inside the organization working directly on the changes along with five executives who provided insight and feedback on content as it was being developed; six people from the web design firm and two people from a company that would proofread all of the new content. In all, at least 18 people helped make the vision of a new website a reality. And the result of everyone's contribution had a nice ending: not only did the new website help advance the company's visibility and drive new business and add-on business with existing clients, it won several design awards.

Besides bringing together and leveraging the skills of the right people, the website redesign project was successful because the company valued the process of selling new ideas. Senior management considered new approaches. A new idea wasn't always given the green light, but it was considered. This practice is brilliantly described in one of the most influential management books ever published, *My Years with General Motors*. According to GM leader Alfred Sloan:

> "The practice of selling major proposals is an important feature of General Motors' management. Any proposal must be sold to central management and if it affects other divisions it must be sold to them as well. Sound management also requires that the central office should in most cases sell its proposals to the divisions, which it does though policy groups and group executives. The selling approach provides an important safeguard ... against ill-considered decisions. It assures that any basic decision is made only after thorough consideration by all parties concerned ... The manager who would like to operate on a hunch will usually find it hard to sell his ideas to others on this basis.

But, in general, whatever sacrifice might be entailed in ruling out a possibly brilliant hunch is compensated for by the better-than-average results which can be expected from a policy that can be strongly defended against well-informed and sympathetic criticism."

(Sloan, 1963; see also Shell and Moussa, 2008)

Nothing convinces like conviction

Let's say you're ready to sell an idea. Based on what you learned in this chapter, you're aware of your communication style and know how to adapt it to others'. You've clarified a problem and crafted a creative solution after researching and testing your ideas. You've "worked your network" and now have the support of the right people. You're ready to make your pitch. I suggest you have one more element in place. You're convinced, enthusiastic, passionate – you deeply believe in – what you're about to propose. With all of the other elements of strategic communication aligned, expressing your solutions with a true and evident conviction gives you as good a chance as possible at winning.

There's no formula for finding enthusiasm about the many possibilities that life and the business world offer. As a child you pick up a camera and start taking photos. You're enthralled with the process and before long you have a makeshift darkroom in the basement. Eventually you become the top salesman for a leading camera manufacturer because your expertise and natural enthusiasm for photography motivate people to buy. Retailers like dealing with you because you care that they succeed and that their customers are happy. Your ability to persuade doesn't even feel like an effort, or a job, because you're convinced that there's nothing better than the art and practice of photography.

From a young age my brother Marc and I have had a passion for music and for enjoying it through the best stereo equipment we could afford. We read high-end sound equipment journals, hung out in the best stores sharing insights and opinions with knowledgeable sales staff and the stores' owners. Through the years to this day we continually upgrade our equipment, always on the hunt for new amplifiers, pre-amplifiers, tuners, CD players and, yes, we still have turntables and play vinyl records that sound amazing when played on a good system.

One day we were in a leading audio equipment store; I was there to purchase some new components. While I was busy with the manager a couple entered the store and started to listen to various speakers they were

considering. During the process they struck up a conversation with Marc. He suggested they listen to a particular brand of speakers that he was passionate about at the time. He discussed how the construction of the speakers was unique, why they were a good buy within the couple's price range and, most importantly, had them sit down and position themselves correctly to fully experience the speakers' sound quality. By the time the manager walked back into the room, they had their credit card out and were ready to take the speakers home.

Without really selling, Marc sold a pair of speakers for the store and the couple went home happy. There were several driving forces behind the transaction. One was that Marc's conviction and enthusiasm motivated the couple to consider the speaker brand. Second, Marc knew his stuff, therefore his opinions seemed reasonable and solid to the couple. Third, these elements created a powerful persuasive force. At some point the couple decided that Marc was trustworthy and that going with his suggested brand would result in a satisfactory purchase. The key word here is "trustworthy." This leads us to the next chapter where I spotlight the one key communication element that, if absent, will cause all persuasive communication efforts to eventually collapse like the proverbial house of cards. That element is credibility.

Notes

1. Rankin offers excellent examples and explanations of the difference between strategic and expressive communication.
2. Shell and Moussa offer a penetrating analysis of the barriers that pose the greatest risks to a successful "influence encounter." I've adapted several of their principles in this chapter.
3. James L. Horton, "The persuasion principles: they haven't changed much." Retrieved 25 July 2013 from *http://www.online-pr.com/Holding/PersuasionPrinciples.pdf* Horton quotes Aristotle as stating in *On Rhetoric*: "It is not true, as some writers assume in their treatises on rhetoric, that the personal goodness revealed by the speaker contributes nothing to his power of persuasion; on the contrary, his character may almost be called the most effective mean of persuasion he possesses."
4. This story is taken from Goodwin (2005) and Shell and Moussa (2008

5

Be credible: why should you believe me?

"The leader must know, must know that he knows; and must make it abundantly clear to others that he knows."

(Clarence B. Randall)

Abstract: There are four important practices that can create a solid foundation for business relationships based on trust and credibility. One is to communicate honestly, which can advance your case by fostering the right impression. Demonstrating your competence is also important. The more capable you appear, the more influence you will have. Third, show respect, a practice that is evident in virtually every successful organization. Fourth, continue to grow, to get better. The best companies and business professionals are not afraid to fail. When they do, they gather feedback, they learn from it and they improve.

Key words: Six Sigma, honesty, brutal honesty, authenticity, talking straight, competence, perceived competence, knowing your stuff, AIIM, show respect, Synovus Financial Corporation, the waiter rule, Brenda Barnes, Tom Watson, Sr., feedback, continuous improvement, fear of failure.

To me, the quote from Clarence B. Randall, author of *Making Good in Management*, is the essence of credibility. There are many ways to define credibility, or trustworthiness, but in my experience knowing your stuff and making it clear to others that you know your stuff is critical. How do you make it clear that you are capable? Communicating plainly backed by certain behaviors that I'll explore in this chapter is a powerful way to make the case that you can be trusted.

Taking the time to understand

Recently I worked with a technology service provider that was competing for an outsourcing contract to take over document-imaging processes for one of the largest insurance companies in the U.S. The service provider took the time to truly understand not only the technical and business needs of the insurance company, but also what the company believed in; what it stood for.

On its website, the insurance company stated that it took pride in being a trusted business partner that delivered excellence through advanced, customer-focused solutions and knowledgeable insight. In a nutshell, the company stood for trust, customer service and expertise. The technology service provider had the same values and set out to win the business by clearly communicating this fact, backed by specific actions. Two of these actions, which the service provider took during the "request for information" phase of the proposal process, were particularly effective.

Two actions that counted

One, the service provider demonstrated its customer-focused approach and professionalism by bringing select insurance company executives to see one of its operations and meet its team working at a client site. This was a way of communicating "don't just listen to what we say but come see us in action, meet our team and talk to one of clients for which we are providing services similar to what we'll implement for you." The insurance executives visited the operation, talked to team members and client executives. As a result, the insurance company was impressed not only with the service provider's technical expertise, but also by its ability to provide creative solutions that utilized one of its offshore document-imaging and coding operations. This was important because it indicated to the insurance company that the service provider could help it realize a vision for the future that included new ways of managing business process workflows.

The other action was based on the fact that the service provider knew the insurance company ideally wanted to manage business processes under a Six Sigma–based model. (Six Sigma is a disciplined, data-driven approach and methodology for eliminating defects and supporting continuous improvement in any process – from manufacturing to transactional and from product to service.) The service provider brought in its Best Practices team to meet with an insurance company team comprised of the company's vice president of quality and two Six Sigma black belts. (A black belt is someone who holds high-level certification in Six Sigma methodology).

"I've heard enough!"

The service provider's Best Practices team asked detailed questions and offered suggestions on how it could use Six Sigma methods to benchmark, monitor and continuously improved the insurance company's document-imaging processes. At one point in the meeting, the company's vice president of quality said "I've heard enough." Often that statement is followed by one you'd rather not hear. In this case the vice president followed up with, "Your team is fantastic." The service provider was given the contract. It proved that its team had the right expertise and could be trusted to get the job done. Credibility won the day.

Communicate honestly

The service provider did many things right in securing the contract. It communicated and acted in ways that lay a solid foundation for a relationship based on trust and credibility. I'll explore several of these ways of communicating and acting in this chapter, starting with the practice of communicating honestly.

I use the word "practice" deliberately because communicating honestly, similar to other practices I'll highlight, seems an almost self-evident and basic common sense approach to business and personal relationships. However, like many things in life, it's more complicated than that. Communicating honestly, with integrity and without spin, is easier in concept than in practice, which in turn is why it's easy to forget its importance. But if you want to advance your cause by leaving the right impression, communicating honestly is critical. Author Stephen Covey concisely summarizes this point: "It's possible to tell the truth and leave the wrong impression. Leaving the right impression means communicating so clearly that you cannot be misunderstood" (Covey, 2006).

As Covey points out, Warren Buffett offers a good example of this practice in the management letter he writes every year for his company's annual report. His communication is straightforward and without spin:

- I've made this kind of deal a few times myself – and, on balance, my actions have cost you money.

- I didn't do that job very well last year. My hope was to make several multibillion dollar acquisitions that would add new and significant streams of earnings to the many we already have. But I struck out.

- Rather than address the situation head-on, however, I wasted several years while we attempted to sell the operation. . . . Fault me for dithering.

(Buffett, 2004–2005)

Is there anything unclear about what Buffett has to say? Is it easy to misunderstand his meaning? I don't think so. His talk is straight and his intent obvious. It's important to remember that while this approach can demand some courage and tact, there's a price in not doing it. That price is resentment, which doesn't help anyone.

Years ago, when I worked for a public relations agency as an account director, I arranged a meeting with a marketing firm to explore ways they might help on a project. I included my bosses, the agency president and vice president in the meeting. Despite the fact that I had arranged the brainstorming session, the two executives from the marketing firm played almost continuously to my bosses. I wasn't entirely ignored, but close to it. Instead of finding a genuine, straightforward way of inserting myself into the interactions, I remained silent and, as you might guess, grew resentful.

Later I mentioned how I felt to the agency's vice president, with whom I had a good relationship. His response was simply that I should have spoken up candidly. I probably would have received a positive response and might have gained an opportunity to move the discussion in different directions and even offer some creative input. He was right. No one, including me, gained anything from my silence.

What do you see?

Communicating honestly means simply stating what you feel, think and see. One of my favorite literary examples of the latter – expressing what you see with your own eyes – is the classic Hans Christian Andersen story, *The Emperor's New Clothes*.

You might recall that in the story the emperor was more interested in showing off his clothes while going to theater, reviewing his soldiers or riding in his carriage, than he was being a good leader. Two swindlers came to the city and figured out a way to use the emperor's obsession to their advantage. They told everyone that they were weavers and could weave the most magnificent fabrics imaginable. Their colors and patterns were not only high quality, but clothes made of their cloth had a way of becoming invisible to anyone who was stupid or "unfit for his office." In the context of this chapter, the swindlers were saying, "If you don't see the clothes made from our cloth you are incompetent, unintelligent and not credible." Their genius was to get people to do the opposite of acting credibly – to not talk straight, to lie and deny what they see with their own eyes.

You may know the rest of the tale. The emperor pays the swindlers a lot of money to weave him a set of clothes. The swindlers set up two looms and pretended to weave, although there was nothing on the looms. The emperor sends one and then another trusted advisor to check on progress while the weavers make the clothes. Neither advisor wants to admit he didn't see anything. They don't want to be viewed as fools. Then the emperor himself visits the swindlers. He also sees nothing but won't admit it to anyone, even himself.

The non-existent garments are eventually finished. The emperor dons them and goes out for a procession in the city streets. No one would confess that the emperor had no clothes on. Finally, someone does speak the plain truth. As the story comes to a close:

> "But he hasn't anything on," a little child said.
> "Did you ever hear such innocent prattle?" said its father. And one person whispered to another what the child had said, "He hasn't anything on. A child says he hasn't anything on."
> "But he hasn't got anything on!" the whole town cried out a last.
> The emperor shivered, for he suspected they were right. But he thought, "This procession has got to go on." So he walked more proudly than ever, as his noblemen held high the train that wasn't there at all.[1]

When you communicate as the child does in the story, without guile or spin, without concern for towing the party or the corporate line, amazing things can happen. Teams become more productive. Meetings are shorter. Motivation increases. Trust is maximized. Results are achieved. Trust is established.

When you communicate as everyone else does in the story, without courage or integrity, without concern that others should know the truth, negative things can happen. Team members are unclear about how to reach goals. Motivation suffers. Trust is low; suspicion high. Resentments build. Productivity grinds to a halt. To paraphrase Andersen, the procession goes on with everyone holding up an enterprise that's not really there at all. Because it's not based on people being honest with each other, the enterprise will likely fail, sooner or later.

As the case history I highlighted earlier attests, demonstrating competence, showing that you "know your stuff," is an important element of credibility and your ability to persuade others. But combining competence with honesty, which supports trustworthiness, may arguably create the most powerful persuasive force of all when it comes to effective communication. In his book *3 Steps to Yes* Gene Bedell opens a chapter with a quote from French revolutionary, writer, diplomat and journalist Honoré de Mirabeau: "If honesty did not exist, we ought to invent it as the best means of getting rich." Bedell then has this to say about trustworthiness:

> "If competence has a peer in persuasion, it's trustworthiness. Persuasion research has confirmed repeatedly that trustworthiness and competence together are by far the most important personal characteristics affecting persuasiveness. All else pales in comparison. Unlike competence, which you may be able to assign to your team's designated expert, you can't delegate trustworthiness. People rely on your representations about your proposal's ability to meet their needs, its costs, and its value, compared with options they must forgo. If they doubt your trustworthiness, what you say won't give them the assurances they need so that the positive buying forces win out against the negative buying anxieties."

> (Bedell, 2000)

Taking it too far

Of course, it's possible to take the principle of honest communication too far. Covey provides an example in the following brief story, again with a child at the center:

> "While straight talk is vital to establishing trust, in most situations, it needs to be tempered by skill, tact, and good judgment. I had this point

burned indelibly into my own mind one time when our family was on vacation at the beach and I decided to go for a swim. When I took off my shirt, my three-year-old daughter looked at me and exclaimed, 'Whoa, Daddy! You have a big tummy!' Unfortunately, that was straight talk – but it was not tempered by any tact or consideration whatsoever!"

(Covey, 2006)

Some leaders, in the name of talking straight, justify condescension and demeaning others. Honesty becomes transformed into "brutal honesty." What you say may be true, but if it's hurtful and expressed without respect for others, they will draw away from you. Your "honesty" and "straightforwardness" will be transformed into a weakness and your chance of success will be greatly diminished.

As I pointed out in the previous chapter, one of the most important keys to effective communication – which includes communicating honestly without hurting relationships – is self-awareness. The key to communicating honestly is to be authentic; that is, simply being who we are. The opposite is to "put on an act," where, because our main concern is how we are seen by others, we behave in ways that we believe are more acceptable and safer.

Deactivate your invisible fence

Writer, consultant and coach Sandy Allgeier likens putting on an act to constructing an invisible fence around ourselves. She states:

"When we activate our invisible fence, we begin to act in a way we believe is either more acceptable to others or one that we perceive to be safe – versus being our true and imperfect selves. We learn to trade in our authenticity for acting because we convince ourselves that our act is more acceptable."

(Allgeier, 2009)

I was once in a taxi cab in New York City that was cut off by another car. The cab driver became enraged, sped up beside the car, lowered his window and prepared to give the other driver a serious piece of his mind. The other driver lowered his window and calmly said, "I'm sorry. I made a mistake. It was my fault." That was it. There was no "let's get ready to rumble" act – just a simple, straight, concise honest admission of a mistake. The transformation in the cab driver was amazing to witness. The fence came down; he smiled, put up his hand in a gesture of conciliation and said, "No problem."

Sandy Allgeier points out that the true measure of being authentic is when we are authentic even in difficult or potentially explosive situations such as the driver who cut off the taxi cab. Allgeier offers an inspiring example of authenticity from the corporate world. Only six months after joining the organization, the president of a business unit of a large financial services company, whom Allgeier refers to as "Rob," was told the business was going to be purchased by a large European firm. It was likely that the business would relocate to Europe and Rob's role as president would be eliminated. He was also asked to help "hold things together" at a difficult time. In reality this meant trying to keep employees focused on their jobs so the company could continue to run successfully. Senior management didn't want a mass exodus of talent, which would impair operations.

Rob decided that there was only one approach that had a chance of working despite the trying circumstances. If he wanted to motivate employees to stay and be productive, he had to be honest, authentic and respectful of them. According to Allgeier:

> "Rob began holding short 'lobby talks' to update employees on the status of the acquisition and the results of the work being done by the transition team. He made statements like: 'I can honestly tell you that I don't know where the business will be located or who will lead it. I will absolutely tell you, however, that I will keep you informed as I learn more.' He also said: 'I know that I have trouble falling asleep some nights, and I'm sure you have the same problem.' He didn't hide his personal concerns, but he also helped employees see the options that might be available for them even if the company did relocate. He did not promise anything, but instead helped employees fully understand what was occurring. He asked for employee commitment and performance during this difficult time – and he committed to doing everything he could do to help them by providing ongoing and honest information."

> (Allgeier, 2009)

Other business units of the same organization heard about and started attending Rob's lobby talks. Many stated that the talks provided the only information they were able to obtain about upcoming acquisition because their own business unit leaders were not communicating about the status of activities. In addition to the updates, employees were drawn to Rob's talks because of his authenticity as a leader. They wanted to hear the truth and they trusted that Rob was giving it to them, to the extent that he could. There was no invisible fence with Rob. Rob's business unit was eventually acquired and moved its operations to Europe. Because there was no president position available to him, Rob left the company. However, his positive impact on more than 1000 employees was significant. He was forthcoming at a time when they needed honesty with no spin or polishing. Rob was a model for authenticity.

Tips for being honest and authentic

Rob's approach of communicating with honesty and authenticity is well within everyone's reach. Following just a few simple practices can help all of us stay authentic in our business and personal relationships. The first tip is based on previous skills I highlighted in Chapter 3 and thus may come as no surprise. Ask yourself a question: What is keeping me from being straight in this moment? One answer might be fear. Fear of not being perceived as competent during a presentation? Fear of making mistakes? Fear that your recommendation for a new records program or IT initiative will not be popular? Whatever the source of your fear, a remedy is to become aware of the benefits of being honest and the disadvantages if you're not.

For example, fear may be holding you back from communicating authentically about your proposal to improve the current records management program. You're concerned that senior management may not like the idea because it will require funds and other resources. You could start your campaign by being straight about the fact that, because it will require budget and personnel, your proposal might not be a popular choice at this time and consequently you were hesitant to suggest the initiative. You can also remind yourself (and key decision makers) that if the proposal isn't seriously considered, a major disadvantage is that the company could suffer in many ways such as not being prepared for potential litigation.

Thus, by simply being clear about the benefits of talking straight about your proposal and keeping in mind the disadvantages if you're not, you'll be less fearful, communicate more credibly and probably increase the likelihood that your proposal will be adopted. Even if it isn't, management will probably appreciate your thoughtfulness and concern for the company. Your trust factor will go up.

Another suggestion for maintaining authenticity is to become aware of how you're feeling during a conversation. Are you "spinning" your communication? The purpose here is not to interrupt the flow of your interaction but to do a simple reality check to determine if you're telling it like it is. Remember the response to the taxi cab driver: "I made a mistake. It was my fault." By being straight, the driver defused a potentially explosive situation. The issue was brought to a close right away. If in becoming aware of your conversation you determine that you are spinning, figure out why and, similar to the previous tip, become clear on the benefits of being honest and the disadvantages of not being upfront.

The third tip for authenticity is based on the first communication skill I spotlighted: be brief. Get to your point quickly. Avoid long-winded preambles, excessive facts or various excuses. Like the response to the taxi cab driver, less is more. As I've heard lawyers put it, "If you're explaining, you're losing." Think of all the things the driver who cut off the taxi cab could have said. "I'm late for an appointment. Traffic is a nightmare. It was impossible to see you. You could have slowed down and let me in." Instead, the driver said a few honest words and everyone moved on.

By asking yourself if you're being straight, becoming aware if you're spinning during a conversation and getting to your point quickly, you can help maintain authenticity in your personal and professional interactions. Your integrity will be clear to others. You'll be on a solid path toward establishing credibility, especially if others see that you "know your stuff."

Knowing your stuff

Besides communicating honestly, the second best practice I'll focus on for being credible is to know your stuff – and to make sure that others "know that you know." The latter is important for ensuring that you'll be perceived as competent, and perceived competence in turn is critical to your persuasiveness.

When people listen to your proposal, as in a sales situation, they are listening to determine if your solution will meet their needs, how much it will cost, why it is better than the competition and why they won't be making a mistake in awarding you the business. They can't feel confident in their decision unless they are convinced that you know your stuff. Therefore the more capable you appear to them, the more influence you will have.

Perceived competence is important in all professions, but particularly so in records management and IT. The reason is that professionals in these fields not only must be competent in the basics of their discipline; their knowledge must incorporate the latest hardware and software solutions as well as industry trends and regulations spanning such areas as compliance and security standards. People need to know that you are proficient in all these and other areas in order to believe you, to put their trust in you.

In fact, perceived competence is so important in IT that professionals such as programmers are often granted different consideration when it comes to personal elements such as appearance and dress. As Gene Bedell points out:

"A lawyer you're consulting comes to our meeting late and shabbily dressed, stares out the window while he's talking to you, and mumbles answers to your questions. Despite three advanced degrees and a colleague's referral, somehow the lawyer's not credible and it's no sale. You end the meeting intent on finding someone else to represent you.

A programmer you're consulting comes to your meeting late and shabbily dressed, stares out the window while he's talking to you, and mumbles answers to your questions. Although he has the same personal characteristics as the lawyer you didn't hire, you find the programmer credible. You agree to an outrageous consulting fee and follow his advice to the letter."

(Bedell, 2000)

Bedell makes the case that the relationship between the personal characteristics of the persuader and persuasiveness is not always straightforward. Two different people can dress the same way in two different situations and the results can be the opposite, in one case negative and in the other positive. The programmer was perceived as technically proficient, therefore credible. Personal characteristics were largely irrelevant.

The key word: "perceived"

A key word in the previous few paragraphs is "perceived." You may in fact be competent in a given area. If that competence is not clear to others, however, you will not have maximum credibility and therefore influence.

Early in my career I worked for several years as an assistant corporate buyer for a major retailer that had numerous stores across the country. An important part of my job was to write internal communications including marketing reports and industry trends analyses. My background at the time also included a Bachelor of Arts degree in English and I had published several articles in industry trade publications.

Enjoying my communications activities more than the world of retail, I decided to make a career transition into public relations. After several interviews with a rising mid-size public relations firm, I was being considered for the job. Despite the fact that I was competent in marketing communications, the firm's CEO wanted to be sure that I knew my stuff. He wanted to be convinced that I could apply my corporate buying experience and writing skills in the public relations field. Consequently he asked me to write and edit several articles and a press release. As a result of my efforts, the CEO believed I was competent and offered me the job, which I accepted.

What if you're not competent?

Life would be easier if people believed you were competent in everything. But you're not and sometimes you need to be persuasive in areas where you fall short in expertise.

You want to motivate your teenage children to eat healthier and exercise. They know that your idea of breakfast is a glazed donut; you know nothing about nutrition and your main exercise is changing channels on the remote control. Tough road ahead.

You apply for a job as head of marketing for a firm that provides document management solutions. Your background includes years of experience marketing consumer goods. Tough road ahead. You may know a lot about document management technology, but the interviewer doesn't believe you're as competent as other candidates.

You are performing mainly administrative duties for the human resources department of an organization and want to advance your career. You are given an opportunity to volunteer on higher level projects that you believe could help you learn more and possibly increase your value to the company. The problem is that you know little about the project topics or how to do the work. Tough road ahead.

Get competent

The good news is that you can become competent and thereby become more persuasive, more trustworthy. You can read, talk to experts, research organizations that offer classes and certifications, watch online tutorials and attend seminars.

If the issue with your children is nutrition and exercise, you can learn about healthy eating and the benefits of supplements by reading books and published research and then share your knowledge with your kids. When they see that your diet has changed, you take vitamins daily and you're going the gym several times a week, you're chances of persuading them increase dramatically.

If you want to direct marketing for a document management solutions provider, you can learn about industry associations that offer courses designed to improve your skills. You find an organization such as AIIM (Association for Information and Image Management) and take an online certification course in electronic content management. You study and pass the exam and are now a certified electronic content management practitioner (ECM Practitioner). The job interviewer now perceives you as credible in document management.[2]

If you want to advance your career in human resources by volunteering on projects in which you have minimal expertise, you get competent by reading. You study manuals and books at night and during lunch breaks. You ask questions of those more experienced. You consume all the information you can about the topics of the projects you're working on. You build your personal credibility by making sure you know your stuff. Eventually, you become vice president of human resources (case history spotlighted in Allgeier, 2009).

Team competence

There is a constant challenge with being competent. You can't be an expert in everything. You're a senior executive at a public relations firm competing for business with a real estate account. Your capabilities and track record in every public relations discipline are impeccable. There's one problem. Your experience in the real estate field is minimal. What can you do? You can bring to the presentation a member of your firm who does have solid real estate expertise. You can team competence. Because your real estate expert would be part of the team working on the account, now your *firm* has credibility, not just you. Your chances of winning the business are much greater.

I can personally relate to this example. While I was director of corporate communications for a technology company, I launched a search for a public relations firm that could help my company increase its visibility and improve sales. After a lengthy process of reading their proposals and asking many questions, I narrowed the field down to three firms that could potentially do the job. They were scheduled to present their programs to me, my boss and our marketing team. One firm stood out and won our business because it was the most credible. It offered expertise in a way that was different from the other firms.

The team of professionals that would work on our account each had a specialty that was important to us and they would only focus on that one specialty. The media relations person would only direct publicity outreach. She wouldn't write or book speaking engagements. The writer would only write. He would craft press releases, articles, speeches, case histories and other content. He wouldn't do any other activity. The social media expert would only concentrate on promoting our company through Twitter, LinkedIn and Facebook. She wouldn't engage in any other activity such as special events. For the latter, as you might guess, they offered a special events expert. She would only maintain a special events calendar and book speaking opportunities such as trade shows and business conferences. Together, the team, and the firm, offered competence that went beyond what any individual could offer.

Gene Bedell writes about the importance of establishing competence through a team.

> "When the senior partner of a law firm that had done an assignment for my company called on me to propose helping us with some trademark issues, he brought with him the head of his firm's intellectual property group. Although I had the highest regard for the senior partner and his firm, he would not have won this additional business without the help of his partner. It made it possible for me to buy based on my perception of his firm's competence in intellectual property natters, not just on my trust in the senior partner."
>
> (Bedell, 2000)

Bedell adds that the team selling approach is particularly important in the technology field, where CEOs and other non-technical officers often meet with prospects who are experts in their specialties and who unreasonably expect that the people calling on them are equally expert. "Worse still, many technologists are quick to brand nontechnical people as lower life forms – plankton on the technology food chain" (Bedell, 2000).

As a high-tech industry CEO, Bedell would never make a call on a prospect or customer without someone from his company who was at least as technically knowledgeable as the smartest person the customer or prospect was bringing to the meeting. He made sure other executives at his company followed the same rule. This approach helped ensure that his *company* was always perceived as technically competent, even if the executive on the call wasn't (Bedell, 2000).

Show respect

In addition to communicating honestly and demonstrating that you know your stuff, a third way to establish your credibility is to show respect. What does it mean to show respect? An anonymous quote I like provides one answer: "You can judge a person's character by the way he treats people who can't help him or hurt him." I believe evidence supports the fact that treating others well not only can underscore credibility, it can help drive success for individuals and organizations. Let's look at an example of the latter.

Synovus Financial Corporation has been recognized as one of *FORTUNE* magazine's 100 Best Companies to work for in America for many years since the rankings began. The company's chairman, James Blanchard, shared what he believed made Synovus and other companies not only successful, but great places to work.

"There's a common thread that runs through those very few organizations that are just bursting out on top all the time. They're meeting and exceeding their goals. They're realizing their visions and aspirations. They're always over and above their expectations ... And yet this group of robust, energized, enthusiastic, continually successful organizations, they seem to have a secret. And frankly, we have studied it, we have gone to school, we have consulted, we've done everything we can to try and find the formula that says, 'We'll be one of these in this very small, select group that seems to achieve perpetual success.'

The secret, the clue, the common thread is simply how you treat folks. It's how you treat your fellow man, and you treat your team members and how you treat your customers, your regulators, your general public, your audiences, your communities. How you value the worth of an individual, how you bring the human factor into real importance and not just a statement you make in your annual report."[3]

What Blanchard refers to as "how you treat folks" is a practice based on the principles of fairness, kindness, love and civility. It's an approach that can create more than business success and a great place to work: it can motivate people to be loyal, to care about contributing to the organization.

One technology service provider I worked with put showing respect for its employees and clients in writing, stating that respecting others was one of its core values. These values are displayed in posters that hang on the walls of its corporate headquarters and at client locations where it provides outsourced IT services. More than displaying posters, the service provider practices what it preaches. It's commitment to showing respect, for example, extends to hiring employees with disabilities and special needs. The company believes that these individuals can make significant contributions to the enterprise.

My wallet was stolen, not my bus pass

One such employee, Chris, was born with Down Syndrome. He worked for an organization that signed an outsourcing contract with the technology service provider, which brought him on board and trained him to work in the mailroom. Chris does three mail runs a day in addition to sorting mail and completing other tasks. In an interview with a human resources magazine, aided by his mother Chris stated "I love my job, am never late or absent, and always treat everyone with kindness and respect."

One day Chris was robbed while waiting for the bus he rides to work. Not deterred, he went to work and called home only to be questioned by his mother as to why he didn't return home immediately after the incident. Chris's response: "My wallet was stolen, not my bus pass." His mother's response: "Heaven forbid you'd let a robbery interfere with you getting to work on time." Only genuine respect and caring for an individual can generate that kind of loyalty.

Like the technology service provider, Chris also does more than talk about respecting and helping others. He enjoys raising money for the annual National Association for Down Syndrome Bowl-A-Thon for which he raised more than $138,000 over the past 25 years. Chris's story brings to mind a statement by Richard Branson, founder and chairman of The Virgin Group: "I try to treat people as human beings ... If they know you care; it brings out the best in them."

The waiter rule

The opposite of showing respect is to fake caring or to demonstrate concern for some (those who can help you) and not others (those who can't). This sneaky approach to respect is sometimes illustrated by what has become known as "the waiter rule." The idea is that you reveal a lot about your concern for others by how you treat a waiter in a restaurant. Former Sara Lee CEO Brenda Barnes, who was once a waitress, said "Sitting in the chair of CEO makes me no better of a person that the forklift operator in our plant. If you treat the waiter, or a subordinate, like garbage, guess what? Are they going to give it their all? I don't think so" (Jones, 2006).

When it came to others, whether a waiter, forklift operator or her own children, Brenda Barnes did more than talk about caring. She lived it and her story is an inspiring example of how concern can make a difference.

"At the height of her career, Brenda Barnes famously quit her big job at Pepsi to be with her kids. Years later, a massive stroke nearly killed her – and her daughter returned the favor.

Brenda Barnes was the most powerful woman in the consumer packaged-goods industry in the '90s when she quit her senior post at PepsiCo to go home to her family. She famously sparked the having-it-all debate – and went on to raise three great kids. Then she became a role model for dropping out and coming back successfully. She did it by joining a slew of prominent boards – Avon, the New York Times, Sears, Starwood Hotels, and Lucasfilm, now part of Walt Disney. Stacking up that board experience, Barnes attracted the favor of recruiters and snagged the top job at Sara Lee, which she led for five years until 2010.

This was when a massive stroke ended Barnes' corporate career. And it could have ended her life. But something amazing happened. Barnes' daughter Erin, who had been nine years old when her mom quit the Pepsi job for her, graduated from Notre Dame the very week her mother had her stroke. Erin decided to quit the job she had lined up at Campbell Soup so she could help her mom recover. Barnes came back to life beyond anyone's expectations. Together, Brenda and Erin redefined power and success."

(Sellers, 2012)

Who cleans your dorm?

For many people the issue is not that they don't value showing respect. It's that our busy, hyperactive, multitasking world of frenetic activity makes it easy to overlook opportunities to be respectful. Every so often an individual or event jolts us into remembering that demonstrating respect and being aware of others truly matters. I shared one personal experience in the previous chapter about my father walking to the back of our local dry cleaner operation to tip the person who pressed his clothes. Here is another example offered by Stephen Covey that signaled a wake-up call for a student taking an exam.

> "I particularly like the story of the business student who did well on her final exam until she came to the last question: 'What is the name of the person who cleans your dorm?' She was incredulous. How could she be expected to know the answer to that? And what in the world did it have to do with her business degree? Finally, she asked the professor if the question really counted on their final grade. 'Indeed it does!' he replied. 'Most of you dream about being president and CEO of a successful company. But success is a team effort. A good leader takes nothing for granted and recognizes the contributions made by everyone on the team – even those people who appear to do the most insignificant jobs'."
>
> (Covey, 2006)

It's interesting to remember, in the context of this chapter, that the purpose of an exam is to demonstrate that you know your stuff; that you are competent in a given subject. One teacher reminded his students that competence extends beyond expertise. It embraces the willingness to recognize others.

I believe the teacher was communicating that competence is not just a "soft" business skill. It has a direct relationship to trust and therefore to the bottom line. And of the business skills that underscore credibility, showing respect may be the easiest to practice. Think about how little it takes to demonstrate that you care. Write a thank-you note. Call people for no other reason than to find out how they are doing. Send emails that demonstrate concern. Tip someone when it's not required. In the spirit of the teacher's exam question, know the name of the person who cleans your dorm.

Continue to grow

Even if you're not a basketball fan, chances are you've heard of Michael Jordan, whose career was full of great accomplishments. Few would deny that he was among the best to ever play the game. Many fans may not be aware that in high school he was 5'10" with average skills, far from the legendary player he would become later at 6'6". In an interview with *Sports Illustrated* Jordan's high-school coach, Clifton Herring, described Jordan at the time this way: "... his shooting was merely good and his defense mediocre."[4] As a result of this assessment and the fact that the high-school team needed taller players, one year Jordan was not selected for the varsity roster and put on Junior Varsity[5] to develop more. According to the *Sports Illustrated* article:

> "The Laney Bucs[6] did have one major weakness, and that was size. They didn't have a returning player taller than 6'3" ... In those days it was rare for sophomores to make varsity. Herring made one exception in 1978, one designed to remedy his team's height disadvantage. That is part of the reason Mike Jordan went home and cried in his room after reading the two lists. It wasn't just that his name was missing from the varsity roster. It was also that as he scanned the list he saw the name of another sophomore, one of his close friends, the 6'7" Leroy Smith."[7]

Jordan evidently gathered himself, moved past his disappointment and focused on getting better. He continued to grow his shooting and defensive skills until he retired. Like any famous athlete, Jordan had his critics throughout his career. He always silenced them by getting better.

> "Michael's response to his critics was simple. He never argued with them or dismissed them; instead he kept quiet and listened. Instead of taking them negatively, Jordan always took them as a challenge. It didn't matter what the criticisms were, Michael would answer his critics by working harder to improve his game. He would take any apparent weaknesses in his game and work them into strengths, and in the process he would prove the critics wrong."[8]

Jordan epitomizes the fourth way to establish your credibility. In addition to communicating honestly, knowing your stuff and showing respect, continue to grow. Others will see your development, note the results you achieve and consequently be more likely to trust you.

How to get better

There are two key ways to continue getting better. One, as Michael Jordan demonstrates, is to learn from your mistakes. Many of the most successful people in business and in life see mistakes as feedback that will help them continually improve. They become experts in learning how to learn from mistakes. They lose the fear of failure. Instead, they view failure as a way to achieve insights and breakthroughs. Albert Einstein stated, "I think and think for months and years. Ninety-nine times the conclusion is false. The hundredth time I am right." In talking about the invention of the light bulb, Thomas Edison said, "I didn't fail ten thousand times. I successfully eliminated ten thousand materials and combinations that didn't work."

The best companies think in a similar way and smart leaders create an environment that encourages risk taking. A good example is IBM founder Tom Watson, Sr. In *Leaders: Strategies for Taking Charge*, Warren Bennis and Burt Nanus tell the following story about Watson:

"A promising junior executive of IBM was involved in a risky venture for the company and managed to lose over $10 million in the gamble. It was a disaster. When Watson called the nervous executive into his office, the young man blurted out 'I guess you want my resignation?' Watson said, 'You can't be serious. We've just spent $10 million educating you'."

(Bennis and Nanus, 1985)

This kind of thinking supports one of Watson's formulas for success. As he once said, "If you want to increase your success rate, double your failure rate."

Records and IT management are complex disciplines that require sophisticated equipment, software and procedures. Mistakes and problems are inevitable. I suggest that the next time you make a mistake, reframe it as feedback. Identify what you learned from it and think about ways you can adjust your approach to get different results. Keep the quotes from Einstein and Edison handy as well as the Jordan and Watson stories, and find others that are meaningful to you. Once you get over the fear of failing you are free to fly as high as you set your sights. That's what Michael Jordan did, literally.

The other way to continue growing – and critical to learning from your mistakes – is to get feedback as often as possible. Seeking feedback and acting on it to improve products and services is one hallmark of a growing, learning and successful company. An avid photo enthusiast,

I almost always shop at the same photography store because of its excellent selection of products and top-quality service. The store also takes the time to send me an email feedback request every time I make a purchase. Whenever I buy a book from Amazon.com, the company asks me to rate every order I place with a third-party seller and my feedback becomes part of the seller's performance rating. Every company I've worked for or consulted with does some form of client feedback survey and makes adjustments based on the input received.

At the beginning of this chapter I related how a technology services provider won significant business because it has expertise in Six Sigma–based performance improvement approaches. These approaches enable enterprises to monitor important processes in near real time, uncover and eliminate defects, and thereby continuously improve virtually any process including records and IT management activities. Six Sigma practices enable organizations to get feedback, learn from "mistakes" that are occurring right now and eliminate them relatively fast. That's a powerful capability in today's global, 24-hour, 7-day-a-week competitive business environment where fixing problems fast is virtually a requirement for success. Six Sigma–based approaches are simply ways of obtaining feedback, which helps many of the world's largest companies get better. Feedback can do the same for you.

Being credible is critical

Being credible is critical to communicating effectively and ultimately getting what you want. I was reminded of this principle while writing this chapter during a conversation with a business colleague, a marketing director who has been with a technology company for six months. Employees with the title of director work in offices that have a window. Her office has only blank white walls. While she misses the natural light that graced her previous office for 10 years, she's not ready to request an office with a window. A savvy professional, she wants to prove herself first – meet her performance goals – before making the request. Then she will have credibility, and a greater chance of getting what she wants.

That is the power of credibility. It helps answer the question with which I opened this chapter – Why should you believe me? – and countless variations of this question that support daily business communication. Why should you buy my product or service? Why should you consider

Table 5.1   Am I credible?

Question	Tips
Am I communicating honestly?	Simply state what you feel, think and see; deactivate your invisible fence; remember *The Emperor's New Clothes*
Do I know my stuff?	Get and stay competent by reading, talking to experts and taking classes; team competence by working with colleagues and business partners; remember the quote: "The leader must know, must know that he knows, and must make it abundantly clear to others that he knows"
Am I showing respect?	Treat people with fairness and civility; don't fake caring or show concern for some and not others; remember "the waiter rule"
Am I continuing to grow?	Practice; get feedback; don't be afraid to fail; remember Michael Jordan

my new program proposal? Why should you consider increasing my department's budget? Why should you give me an office with a window?

The questions and tips in Table 5.1 are designed to help you remember how to be credible and stay credible.

At this point we've examined five elements that, together, build a momentum that creates a powerful force. The elements are being brief, clear, receptive, strategic and credible. The force is persuasiveness, the communication talent that brings all the other skills together. Mastering persuasiveness gives you the best chance of attaining your goal. Want to increase your powers of persuasion? The next chapter will show you how.

Notes

1. Hans Christian Andersen, *The Emperor's New Clothes*. Retrieved 23 August 2013 from *http://www.andersen.sdu.dk/vaerk/hersholt/ TheEmperorsNewClothes_e.html*
2. This example is based on personal experience as I hold an ECM Practitioner certification. For more information on AIIM and its certification courses visit *www.aiim.org*
3. James Blanchard speech at the Beta Gamma Sigma International

Honoree Luncheon, 25 April 2005. Retrieved 10 September 2013 from *http://www.betagammasigma.org/exchange/summer05/blanchard.htm*

4. Brian Mazique, "Michael Jordan's high school coach exposes another MJ myth." Retrieved 15 September 2012 from *http://bleacherreport.com/articles/1020151-michael-jordans-high-school-coach-exposes-another-mj-myth*

5. Junior varsity players, though team members, are not the main players in American football, basketball or baseball games.

6. The Laney Buccaneers are an American football team from Wilmington, North Carolina.

7. Brian Mazique, "Michael Jordan's high school coach exposes another MJ myth." Retrieved 15 September 2012 from *http://bleacherreport.com/articles/1020151-michael-jordans-high-school-coach-exposes-another-mj-myth*

8. Andy Huang, "The evolution of Michael Jordan." Retrieved 15 September 2013 from *http://thebestten.wordpress.com/2010/02/09/chapter-35-michael-and-his-critics/*

6

Be persuasive: are you persuaded yet?

"We are generally better persuaded by the reasons we discover ourselves than by those given to us by others."

(Blaise Pascal)

Abstract: Persuasiveness incorporates the other five skills highlighted in this book. Being persuasive can make a huge difference in getting your ideas accepted. While there is no ultimate formula for achieving persuasiveness, there are three elements, or "factors," that can significantly increase your ability to influence others. These include the experience factor, the story factor and the confidence factor. Great presenters from Winston Churchill to Steve Jobs were masters of all three. The key to these factors, particularly confidence, is to continually engage in a specific form of practice: deliberate practice. It is this form of practice over time – more than innate talent – that breeds experts and champions.

Key words: persuasiveness, influence, non-verbal behavior, emotional experience, generate an experience, tone of voice, body language, storytelling, Steve Jobs, rule of three, seeing is believing, expertise, practice, deliberate practice, Winston Churchill, public speaking, Toastmasters International, *Harvard Business Review*, presentation skills, sensory perception, face-to-face communication.

Persuasiveness is one of the most important business communication skills for records and IT managers because they devote so much energy and time motivating others – to accept new ideas, adopt solutions, consider proposals, increase budgets and more. A central point about persuasiveness that I'll repeat several times in this chapter is that if you're talking about yourself (your company, your solution, your expertise, your proposal), you're engaging in a monologue. You won't be persuasive. You may believe what you're saying with all your heart and your listener may appear to be interested, but monologues don't motivate. If, on the other hand, you start talking about your listener's needs, wants and challenges, you're on the right path. Instead of a monologue, now you're ready to truly communicate. But, first, you need to get your listener's attention. He may be in the room or on the phone, but his mind may be miles away. To capture his interest, you need to do something different. As an example that will help you improve your own persuasiveness, I'll tell you a short story. I call it the "saga of the sonic jacket."

Saga of the sonic jacket

Early in my career I worked as a senior account manager for a public relations firm. One of my clients was a leading consumer electronics company that just launched a quirky but interesting product called the Sonic Jacket. The product combines a windbreaker-style jacket with batteries, loudspeakers and a cassette or CD player. At the time (more than 20 years ago), one of the company's executives described the product's rationale this way: "People are taking their music with them, so forward-thinking designers thought, 'Why not build a music system into our clothing to keep the hands free?' "

To me, the Sonic Jacket was a wonder to behold. It had pockets in the front that house four C-size batteries and a cassette or CD player. Five feet of wires sealed into the jacket's Velcro lining are connected to four speakers, two in the lining of the chest pockets and two in the shoulders. The result: you plugged in your CD player and walked around with music emanating from your jacket. You could strut down the boulevard as a human boombox. My question at the time was, "How can I persuade the media to promote the Sonic Jacket?"

After thinking it through, I tailored my message to one publication, a national newsweekly with a column that featured interesting new high-tech products and services. If I could persuade the editor to feature the jacket, I believed that the publication's stature and huge circulation would motivate other media outlets to cover it. To be successful I had to get the editor's attention. I had to do something different, such as entice him to experience the jacket.

After crafting a message that was brief (about 30 seconds to relate because if you can't get an editor's attention right away you're done), direct and strategic (tailored to the editor's interests) I called the editor. I basically said the following (avoiding a monologue about "my" product and stressing why "you" might be interested): "I'm familiar with *your* column and notice that you feature new tech products that are different. I believe I have one that *you* and *your* readers will find fascinating. It's called the Sonic Jacket. It has speakers and wires built into the lining. *You* put your CD into one of the jacket's pockets, attach it to one of the wires and *voilà*, *you* walk around, hands free, with music playing. To really appreciate the jacket, I think *you'll* want to see it. I can walk over to *your* office whenever *you're* free so you can experience it *yourself*." The editor invited me to his office. The game was on.

The experience is the message

Wearing the Sonic Jacket, I arrived at the editor's office, shook his hand and said a few words about the product. He looked intrigued. I didn't say too much because my strategy was that the experience would be the message. I turned the jacket on; a pop band came to life, singing out of the lining of my jacket and filling the room with music. His eyes lit up and he chuckled at the inventiveness of human beings. Then something magical happened. Writers and columnists put down their phones, locked their computers, came out of their cubicles and gathered around me to marvel at the latest high-tech breakthrough. More eyes lit up, the sound of laughter and jokes mingled with the music. Everyone loved it. The editor asked a few questions, jotted down a few notes and the event was over in about ten minutes. I went back to my office, fingers crossed, hoping that the Sonic Jacket would be featured in next week's column. It was.

My 15 minutes of fame

The day after the column ran Financial News Network called me for a quote and then featured the Sonic Jacket in a new products section. The day after that, CNN called. Then the local newspaper in the town where the consumer electronics manufacturer was headquartered featured the product. The national wire services ran a column on the Sonic Jacket. Publicity momentum for the Sonic Jacket took off, maintained a steady pace for several weeks and then, at least for me, reached a pinnacle. A local TV news show called and asked if they could send a crew to my office to tape a segment of me talking about and demonstrating the Sonic Jacket. The segment would air that night. My 15 minutes of fame, and that of the Sonic Jacket, was kicking in.

The news segment went well and the publicity coverage continued for several more weeks. When the stories died down I did an analysis of the coverage, including the print circulation and broadcast viewership figures. The Sonic Jacket was an unqualified media sensation. My strategy had worked far better than I had anticipated. Why had it worked so well? Keep that question in mind. I will come back to it as we examine some key factors of persuasiveness.

The power of persuasion

Being persuasive gives you power. The dictionary defines "persuasive" as "having the power to induce action or belief." The opposite of being persuasive is to be "unconvincing," which the dictionary characterizes as "not being able to inspire action or belief." Possessing the former – the skill to induce action or belief – can make a huge difference in getting your target audiences, including senior and middle management, to accept your records and IT management proposals.

Key to understanding, and leveraging, the power of persuasion is to remember that it incorporates all the other five skills we've examined. Being persuasive also means being clear, direct, brief, strategic and credible. Imagine trying to be persuasive without one of these skills. Without being clear, what are the chances of persuading the leadership team of your company to approve costs for increasing the records management staff and training programs? My guess is close to zero. Without taking a strategic approach, can you effectively sell your IT solution to an existing client or prospect? I don't think so. Besides incorporating all of the other communication skills, there are three other elements to consider in our goal to master persuasiveness. Let's consider them.

The experience factor

The statement "seeing is believing" makes the point that you are more apt to believe something if you can experience it with your senses. Think about how much daily interaction centers around people trying to persuade other people to do something. Parents try to get children to clean up their room. Entrepreneurs try to motivate individuals and financial organizations to invest millions of dollars in their enterprise. Job candidates try to motivate potential bosses to hire them. Records and IT managers try to get management to consider new initiatives.

One of the most important elements to success in these and countless other scenarios has less to do with logic or data, and much more with creating the right emotional experience. That was certainly the case for me with the Sonic Jacket. Half the battle in motivating the editor to write about the product was won during the first few minutes he saw the jacket and heard pop band harmonies radiating from its lining. I didn't realize it at the time, but I had followed an important principle of persuasiveness in promoting the Sonic Jacket: show, don't tell.

An excellent example of this principle is spotlighted by Brian Fugere, Chelsea Hardaway and John Warshawsky in *Why Business People Speak like Idiots*:

> "In 2003, the film remake of *The Italian Job* was released. This high-speed caper flick, a remake of the 1969 classic, featured the beautiful Charlize Theron. Co-starring, and almost as beautiful, was a fleet of BMW Mini Coopers. Like Theron, the Minis were shown cavorting around Los Angeles doing all sorts of fun, daring maneuvers. The shots highlighted not only the performance of the Minis, but also their playful personality. In later research, BMW learned that sales increased 20 percent in markets where the film was shown.
>
> Notice what the filmmakers didn't do. They didn't assert anything about the Mini. They didn't talk about dual-cone synchronizers, equal-length drive shaft, or four-sensor independent channel anti-lock brakes. They simply demonstrated. They let the car do the talking for them.
>
> We all need to take a cue from *The Italian Job*. Demonstrate, don't assert."
>
> (Fugere et al., 2005)

That's exactly why the Sonic Jacket generated a sonic boom of publicity coverage: because I started the campaign by simply demonstrating it. I let the jacket do the talking (or in this case the "singing") for the manufacturer. Instead of talking about the jacket I generated an experience, which leads me to my next point.

Generate an experience

AmyK Hutchens, an authority on brain research, business communication and leadership, says that the more senses you touch, the better your audience's recollection of an event or meeting will be (Hutchens, 2002).

What most people recall from a meeting is not what you said or what you looked like. It's the experience of how you made them feel. As Hutchens points out, the more vivid your communication the more likely you are to make them feel positive about themselves and receive your message. I call this generating a memorable experience and it can enable you to better connect with people. Hutchens explains that this has to do with the way your brain is wired.

> "In addition to repetition, what else makes connections fuse together so you remember and recall information? You are a sensory being absorbing the world around you through sight, sound, taste, touch, smell and intuition. You remember information that contains intense sensory associations. The taste of your favorite grandmother's recipe, the sight of your uncle's bright and outrageous shirts, the sight of your sister's smile, the sound of an older neighbor's whistling, the touch of a dog's tongue licking your hand. Any sensory perception that is intense and possibly repeated is remembered.
>
> Your brain also thrives on the new and distinctive for you are a naturally curious, eager learner. Anything that is outstanding or different stands out in your mind because it is unusual and unexpected. Your mind is literally more engaged by the novel experience because new connections and associations are being created."
>
> (Hutchens, 2002)

Touching the senses, stimulating positive emotions, creating novel experiences that will linger in the minds of your audience and repeating your message are not abstract scientific concepts that have little to do with persuasive business communication and effective sales skills. On the contrary, Hutchens makes a convincing case that knowing how the brain functions is critical to maximizing your persuasive talents, which in turn can increase your personal and professional success.

Let's sell some software

Let's look at a practical example. Imagine that instead of managing IT activities for your organization, you are selling software. Here's what Hutchens would suggest:

"Suppose you are selling a new software application. When introducing the product it is important to explain how the application complements the buyer's needs and seamlessly fits the type of work performed in her industry. Provide examples. Now you're making it personally relevant.

Next, what's the emotion attached to the purchase? Is it going to create better solutions and thus make her feel better for providing superior answers to her customers? Is it going to reduce time and make her more efficient in the eyes of her customers and/or make her feel better for being more productive? Is it going to cut costs and make her feel better about meeting her budget and increasing her profit margins? Is it going to build customer relations and hence make her feel good about building her business and growing her company's reputation? Is it going to reduce her stress and as a result make her feel better because it reduces her number of headaches? Identify the emotion, address it and leave the buyer feeling good about herself when working with you.

Appeal to the buyer's senses. Let her see the software application (visual). Let her manipulate various technical functions (touch). Let her listen to the solutions it provides as cited by you as well as any sounds directly emitted from the software itself (sound). Let her voice, in her own words, say the benefits she thinks the application will provide for her."

(Hutchens, 2002)

Hutchens' formula for persuasively selling software is equally relevant to promoting a records or IT program within your organization. Make your proposal relevant, identify the main emotion attached to your solution (e.g., management will feel better about reducing risk and enhancing compliance) and appeal to your audience's senses (e.g., let them see and hear a short video about a company in your industry that gained solid business benefits by adopting a similar program). Even if your program doesn't get approved, chances are that management will be impressed by your persuasiveness. They'll take notice. Your credibility will increase. You will have paved the way for future victories. Knowing something now about how the brain functions, the next piece of research won't come as a surprise. In face-to-face communication, studies show that while words are important, tone of voice and body language are also very important because they touch more senses. They also have a far greater impact on the extent to which people will like you while you're delivering a message. This makes vocal tone and body language powerful tools in helping you generate a positive experience in which people feel good about what you're communicating.

Are you congruent?

Albert Mehrabian, a UCLA professor, conducted a series of studies in the 1970s on the relative importance of different types of communication in conveying meaning (Fugere et al., 2005)[1] In his studies, Mehrabian comes to two conclusions. First, that there are basically three elements in any face-to-face communication: words, tone of voice and non-verbal behavior (e.g., facial expression). Second, the non-verbal elements are particularly important for communicating feelings and attitude, especially when they are incongruent: If words disagree with the tone of voice and non-verbal behavior, people tend to believe the tonality and non-verbal behavior.

According to Mehrabian, the three elements account differently for our liking the person who communicates a message concerning their feelings: words account for 7%, tone of voice accounts for 38%, and body language accounts for 55% of our liking.

For effective and meaningful communication about emotions, these three parts of the message need to support each other – they have to be "congruent." In case of any incongruence, the receiver of the message might be irritated by two messages coming from two different channels, giving cues in two different directions.

An example of incongruence in verbal and non-verbal communication:

- Verbal: "I don't have a problem with your ideas for the website redesign."

- Non-verbal: person avoids eye-contact, looks anxious and has a closed body language.

It becomes more likely that the receiver will trust the predominant form of communication, which to Mehrabian's findings is non-verbal (38 + 55%), rather than the literal meaning of the words (7%). This is known as "the 7–38–55% rule."

Are you presenting by rote?

Mehrabian's research is particularly important when we consider how many presenters obsess on that 7 percent – the verbal script. But there's a reason why public speaking and presentation coaches don't want you deliver your content by rote. This approach strips out your personality and instead of enriching the experience for others can deaden it. You can read through 50 PowerPoint slides flawlessly, but chances are that a large portion of your audience tuned out by slide 10 because they noted the apathy in your voice and the fact that you made very little eye contact with any listeners.

The world of entertainment is full of successful celebrities who have a laser-like focus on what they wear, how they sound and how they use body language during interviews and public appearances. They are masters at getting us to pay attention and remember them. This kind of charisma is less common in business, but there are business leaders who do get us to pay attention and to care about what they say. We consider their opinions, follow their careers and buy their products because when they present, they create an emotional experience that's like a force field. We tune out any distraction and entranced, we listen. In my opinion, one of the best communicators in business who exemplifies every skill highlighted in this book was Apple CEO Steve Jobs. His presentations have become the stuff of legend. Let's look at a few reasons for this.

The Jobs' formula

Steve Jobs gave many memorable presentations. Two that I especially like and have studied include his 2005 Stanford commencement speech and his introduction of the iPhone at the 2007 Macworld conference in San Francisco. Both his Stanford speech and iPhone presentation – readily available on YouTube – are mesmerizing and follow a specific formula that you can adapt for your management presentations, conference seminars, webinars and company launch events.[2] While the content and purpose of the iPhone presentation and Stanford address differ, the method of Jobs' delivery followed the same pattern that characterized his best performances. In the next few sections I highlight key elements of his formula and offer some comments on how you might adapt it to hone your own communication skills.

Set the theme

"We are going to make some history today." Jobs opened Macworld 2007 with those words. That was his theme, which he used to build anticipation and hint that a revolutionary new product would be unveiled (the iPhone).

If you just heard that you're about to participate in an historic event, wouldn't you start paying attention? He opened Macworld 2008 with the theme "There is something in the air tonight," which also hinted at the key product announcement, the super thin MacBook Air laptop. In his Stanford commencement speech, Jobs began by stating that he would tell three stories from his life: "That's it; no big deal, just three stories."

Setting the theme gives the audience a guide, a roadmap of what to expect. Once you identify your theme, remember to deliver it several times during your presentation.

Follow the rule of three

People can only absorb so much information in their short-term memory during a presentation. That's why Jobs' presentations always had three or four message points. In the beginning of the iPhone launch, Jobs stated that Apple was going to launch three innovative products: a widescreen iPod with touch controls, a revolutionary new phone and a breakthrough Internet communications device. He repeats this three times. Then the audience gets it and starts cheering wildly. These three products are really one product: the iPhone.

The rule of three is a communications principle that suggests that things that come in groups of three are inherently funnier, more effective and more memorable than other numbers of things. Readers and listeners are more likely to absorb your message or story if it is structured in groups of three. For example: *The Three Stooges, Three Little Pigs, Goldilocks and the Three Bears.*

Following the rule of three will make it much easier to deliver your message and ensure that it will be remembered. If you're suggesting a new IT initiative, build your presentation around the three most important ways it will benefit your company.

Create an unforgettable experience

Creating an experience is what this chapter is all about. Jobs was masterful at generating high-impact moments. In fact, most of Steve Jobs' presentations built up to one big scene. In his 2008 Macworld keynote, his theme of "there's something in the air tonight" comes to life in one such scene in which Jobs says that the MacBook Air is so thin that it will fit in an envelope. He then drew cheers by opening a manila interoffice envelope, pulling out the laptop and holding it up for everyone to see.

What will be the one memorable moment in your next presentation? Decide on it ahead of time and plan how to build up to it.

Express feelings

Earlier I pointed out that to communicate meaningfully, three parts of your message – words, tone of voice and body language – need to be congruent; they need to match. Watch any Jobs' presentation video and you'll see that when he says he's excited about what he's about to unveil, he expresses that excitement from the beginning to the end of the performance through his words, voice and gestures. He uses words like "extraordinary," "amazing," "revolutionary," "unbelievable" and "cool."

At the iPhone launch he describes the phone's design as "something wonderful for the hand." When he demonstrates how to select and play music through the iPhone, you can see the enthusiasm in his face and hear it in his voice as he says "unbelievable" when some of his favorite Beatles and Bob Dylan tunes play over the loudspeakers.

Many speakers get into presentation mode believing that they have to strip out any expressions of true feelings or moments of fun. Nothing could be further from the truth. If you're not enthusiastic about what you're communicating, how can you expect your audience to be?

Tell stories

It should come as no surprise at this point that the three stories Jobs shared at his Stanford commencement speech each had a theme. The first story, "connecting the dots," was about his early life from birth through adoption and going to college. In relating the significant events of these years, Jobs makes the point that you can't know their meaning while they're happening. You can't connect the dots going forward, only looking backward. Therefore, you have to trust that the dots will connect in your future, which gives you confidence to pursue your dream.

The second themed story, "love and loss," highlighted the years he built Apple, was forced out by the Apple board, discovered how much he still loved what he did and then eventually returned to lead Apple again years later.

The final story, "live each day as if it's your last," was about his brush with death when doctors first discovered a tumor on his pancreas.

The point: stories communicate powerfully because they bypass logic and directly touch the emotions. Don't be afraid to tell stories. They can breathe life into your presentations, no matter what the topic.

Build a memorable closing

At the end of his iPhone presentation, Jobs pointed out that the main elements of Apple's product mix – the Mac, iPod, Apple TV and now the iPhone – the only one people still think of as a computer is the Mac. Therefore, the company was changing its name from Apple Computer to Apple Inc. They were dropping "computer" from the name so it would more accurately describe the company's strategy and direction. The audience felt they had been part of a significant moment.

At the end of his Stanford commencement address, Jobs told a story about the *Whole Earth Catalogue*, a counterculture catalog published between 1968 and 1972. When the publication put out its final issue in the mid-1970s, the back page featured an image of a country road with the statement "stay hungry, stay foolish." Jobs ends his address by saying to the graduating students: "Stay hungry, stay foolish. That's what I wish for you." Those words are hard to forget. They speak to feelings, not to logic.

Leave your audience with something that lingers, something they're likely to remember.

The story factor

One essential component of the Jobs' formula, and the second key element of persuasiveness that I'll spotlight in this chapter, is telling stories. Facts, figures, timelines, revenue projections, budget estimates, return on investment calculations and industry research all count. But if you want your audience to accept these details, and ultimately buy into your proposal, nothing beats the power of a story. Leading with a story that effectively and subtly expresses your message can generate feelings in your listeners and thereby influence them to consider the facts and figures that follow.

Watch any Steve Jobs' product launch presentation and long before he brings up any slides containing facts and projections, he has told a number of stories. These tales go right to his audience's feelings and induce excitement, wonder, laughter and anticipation at buying and owning the product. His stories are verbal (an emotional homage to the team that made the product possible), visual (a slide with no words, just a beautiful product photo) and theatrical (taking a tiny product out of his back pocket and showing how it holds a thousand songs, slipping an ultra thin computer out of an interoffice envelope).

In contrast, how many company, industry and general business presentations have you attended in which the presenter basically offered facts and figures? No stories. No building up to a significant, memorable moment. No high-impact closing. You've attended these presentations. You just don't remember them.

Give them a new story

One of the reasons stories are so important to delivering your message is that people come to your presentations with their own stories. These stories might be "records management is not critical to our core business so we should allocate budget elsewhere" or "we're spending too much money on IT and we should consider outsourcing some functions." Author Annette Simmons offers one of the key reasons stories are so important to persuasive communication.

"A good story helps you influence the interpretation people give to facts. Facts aren't influential until they *mean* something to someone. A story delivers a context so that your facts slide into new slots in your listeners' brains. If you don't give them a new story, they will simply slide new facts into old slots. People already have many stories they tell themselves to interpret their experiences. No matter what your message, they will search their memory banks until they find a story that fits for them. Inevitably, the story they pull up will support their current action or inaction – whatever it is that you hope to change. It may be 'all consultants are greedy,' 'everyone in IT is a geek,' or 'poor people just don't want to work.' If you deliver 'facts' (this consultant is not greedy, I'm in IT and I feel your pain, or here is a poor person who wants to work) without giving them a new story, they will tend to discount or bend your facts to fit the existing story. You can rant and rave all you want over people who 'won't face the facts' or who 'ignore the facts' or who 'don't live in the real world,' but your facts won't reach them until you give them a new story."

(Simmons, 2006)

People are not rational

People come to your presentations, meetings or discussions with their own stories, ready to filter your data through those stories. This is one reason you should offer them a new story. There is another. Simmons reminds us that, despite what we think (i.e., despite our own story) people are not rational. Most of the time they make decisions based on feelings, hunches and intuitions. The persuasive communicator knows this and uses "data" to tell stories that touch your feelings before giving you the numbers and other details. Recall Steve Jobs' approach: the slides with revenue projections and competitive analyses come later in the presentation; after you're wild with enthusiasm for the dazzling new product he has pulled out of his back pocket and demonstrated for you.

In the following passage, Simmons reminds us that people are not rational. (Note how she cites recent brain research and bear in mind AmyK Hutchens' emphasis on the importance of generating positive emotions.)

"A storyteller embraces, as a central theme, that people aren't rational and uses what she knows about feelings and emotions. She knows that our choices are primarily driven by our feelings. And she uses 'fact' to find stories that influence how people feel before she gives them data. Recent studies of how the brain works demonstrate that emotions guide and direct our thoughts and our interpretation of rational facts.

There is ample research to document that decisions are based more on feelings than rational, logical thinking. People decide they like a piece of art because someone they like likes it. They will attribute trustworthiness to an individual they have never met because they have seen his or her picture frequently enough for that person to feel familiar. They will select one item out of ten identical items and give a list of rational-sounding reasons why it is superior to the other nine – even though the item is exactly the same as the other nine. For each of these feeling-based decisions (they had no facts) research subjects always made up rational-sounding reasons and believe the reasons they made up. People irrationally believe they are rational."

(Simmons, 2006)

The real estate executive story

Let's experience the difference a story can make in persuasively communicating a fact or rational statement. In the next few sections I'll tell three stories. To quote Steve Jobs: "That's it; no big deal, just three stories." And like Jobs, I'll give each story a title or theme. The first story, about an event that happened early in my career working for a public relations agency, I call "the real estate executive story."

I could say to you, "money doesn't buy happiness." I could support that statement by citing research and facts that help make the statement credible. Having heard the statement many times before, you might agree with my assertion; you might not. But chances are you'll forget my message in a few minutes. However, before making the statement, I could tell you this story.

While serving as senior vice president for a public relations agency in New York City, I brought in a new account; a commercial real estate firm. In preparation for a publicity launch, I called the CEO, Bob, who is intelligent, driven and constantly crafting big deals. I scheduled a meeting to have his photo taken for a press kit. Arriving at his office, I shook Bob's hand as he continued to take numerous calls. By the look on his face, every call was serious business. Bob didn't become a multi-millionaire by resting easy. He was a major player in the New York commercial real estate market, widely known and admired in many social circles and he lived in a palatial condominium with breathtaking views of the city skyline. I know because I met with him there while we planned and discussed the program I was launching. Bob had a son, Eric, who worked with him at the firm, was married to a lovely woman and had achieved market success in his own right. Bob appeared to meet just about any standard we might offer to describe the word "success."

While the photographer was setting up, I told Bob our plan. We'd take a few pictures of him sitting at his desk and have him back working and making deals in about 20 minutes. When the photographer was ready, Bob asked his assistant to hold all his calls and sat up straight in his chair. All of us were ready. I chatted with Bob for a few seconds to get him to relax and then asked him to smile. Then something stunning happened; or didn't happen. Bob tried to smile, but he couldn't. For a time he moved his facial muscles up, down, left and right. He even said at one point, "Hold for a second. I think I feel the smile coming." He wasn't joking. This was an effort for him. The photographer glanced at me and with an imperceptible nod of my head I indicated I agreed: this wasn't going to happen. Bob couldn't smile. I told Bob we were done, thanked him and noticed the relief on his face now that the ordeal was over and he could get back to work.

A little while later I sat back at my own desk. I decided I would tell him I wasn't happy with the way the photos turned out. We could reschedule the shoot or opt to leave the photos out of the press kit. I anticipated his decision: let's forgo the photos. I then thought about what had just transpired and felt sad. I liked and admired Bob. It didn't seem possible that he had so much of what we fight to achieve, but couldn't smile.

Perhaps now if I say "money doesn't buy happiness," the statement seems achingly real to you, as it was to me on that day. Suddenly it's no longer a theoretical concept, a well-worn cliché. A man who had all the trappings of success could not smile. The emotional truth of that "fact" can only be experienced through a story. Just stating it doesn't come close.

The cheap video story

I could assert that "seeing is believing." I could reinforce that statement with some data in an effort to persuade you. Having heard the statement perhaps countless times in your life, you might agree with my statement; you might not. Chances are you won't think much about it. However, before making the statement, I could share this story with you.

> "A team was working with a large retailer on its customer-returns policy. Basically the problem was that the official policies designed by those know-it-alls at headquarters were being ignored everywhere outside of headquarters. Shocking!
>
> So in doing the review, the team went out to all the stores and found tons of evidence that the policies weren't being followed. Loads of charts and graphs. Enough numbers to torture even Fibonacci. When they made the presentation to management, no one bought it.
>
> So the team bought a cheap video camera and went back out to some of the stores. They filmed interviews with eight sales reps, who cheerily offered up their own versions of the returns policy. These were about as on-target as eight darts thrown by eight blindfolded drunks late at night, but at least the acting was within budget. The bumpy, grainy, totally

unprofessional video lasted about four minutes and took less than 5 percent of the time and effort that the rest of the analysis did. And of course it had a profound effect on management, who immediately decided to launch a major effort to fix the problems.

The video team didn't even try to cover everything or nail all the facts. They didn't attempt to present an unbiased case. But seeing is believing. Eight real live people telling simple stories was infinitely more powerful than reams of data."

(Adapted from Fugere et al., 2005)

Now if I start to explain the power of using the concept "seeing is believing" in order to significantly advance your persuasive communication skills, you might feel excited about the power of its possibilities. Perhaps you visualize a way to breathe life into an upcoming presentation. You see a more effective way to promote your company's IT solutions by incorporating customer testimonial videos into your website. But it's no longer an abstract idea. A team changed management's mind about a problem with the company's customer-returns policy by telling the story through video. Once executives felt the emotional impact of the problem, they acted. Just seeing charts and graphs hadn't done the job.

The locked-in-a-boxcar story

I could say to you that our thoughts and expectations yield tremendous power and influence over our lives. I could back up that statement with the most recent studies. Having heard that principle many times before, you might politely nod in agreement. Perhaps you found the research mildly interesting. Within a minute, you go back to concentrating on your cup of coffee. Before talking about the power of belief, however, I could share this story with you.

"Nick was a big, strong, tough man who worked in the railroad yards for many years. He was one of his company's best employees – always there on time, a reliable, hard worker who got along well with the other employees. But Nick had one major problem. His attitude was chronically negative. He was known around the railroad yards as the most pessimistic man on the job. He perpetually feared the worst and constantly worried, fretting that something bad might happen.

One summer day, the crews were told that they could go home an hour early in order to celebrate the birthday of one of the foremen. All the workers left, but somehow Nick accidentally locked himself in a refrigerated boxcar that had been brought into the yard for maintenance. The boxcar was empty and not connected to any of the trains.

When Nick realized that he was locked inside the refrigerated boxcar, he panicked. Nick began beating on the doors so hard that his arms and fists became bloody. He screamed and screamed, but his coworkers had already gone home to get ready for the party. Nobody could hear Nick's desperate calls for help. Again and again he called out, until finally his voice was a raspy whisper.

Aware that he was in a refrigerated boxcar, Nick guessed that the temperature in the unit was well below freezing, maybe as low as five or ten degrees Fahrenheit. Nick feared the worst. He thought, 'What am I going to do? If I don't get out of here, I'm going to freeze to death. There's no way I can stay here all night.' The more he thought about his circumstances, the colder he became ...

To pass the time, he decided to chronicle his demise. He found a pen in his shirt pocket and noticed an old piece of cardboard in the corner of the car. Shivering almost uncontrollably, he scribbled a message to his family. In it Nick noted his dire prospects: 'Getting so cold. Body numb. If I don't get out soon, these will probably be my last words.'

And they were.

The next morning, when the crews came to work, they opened the boxcar and found Nick's body crumpled in the corner. When the autopsy was completed, it revealed that Nick had indeed frozen to death.

Now, here's a fascinating enigma: The investigators discovered that the refrigeration unit for the car in which Nick had been trapped was not even on! In fact, it had been out of order for some time and was not functioning at the time of the man's death. The temperature in the car that night – the night Nick froze to death – was sixty-one degrees. Nick froze to death in slightly less than normal room temperature because he believed he was in a freezing boxcar. He expected to die! He was convinced that he didn't have a chance. He expected the worst. He saw himself as doomed with no way out. He lost the battle in his own mind."

(Osteen, 2004)[3]

After experiencing this story you might feel very different about the idea that thoughts wield power over our lives. We've just had that "fact" communicated in a way that's unforgettable. Hearing the account of someone who died because he was convinced of something that wasn't true shakes us into contemplating how our own unquestioned beliefs might be inviting negative outcomes – in our personal and business lives. For the latter category, we've often heard how important it is for a business professional, whether a budding entrepreneur or battle-tested corporate CEO, to think positively, dream big and never give up. Don't give into negative thinking. Now we might have a new appreciation for the wisdom of this advice.

Three stories you should know how to tell

Not all stories need to be as dramatic or even as long as the examples I just offered. But they need to be meaningful to your audience if you want to win them over. This is particularly the case where your time to present might be limited and the executives seated in front of you might not be overly receptive to what you're about to offer. To give yourself a fighting chance, there are three types of stories you should be able to tell and adapt appropriately to the situation. These stories are: "this is why you can trust me," "this is who I am," and "this is why I am here." Let's look at an example of a "trust story."

As long as I'm still standing

People want to have faith in you as a leader or an expert who can help them succeed. They want to believe in you – your goals, your ability, your vision; they want to believe in the story you tell. I once had to address a group of people who were in a program to improve their public-speaking skills. Many of them were very uncomfortable just standing in front of a group, much less giving a presentation or speech. Having gone through years of similar training myself, I wanted them to trust not only me, but my message that the program and their commitment to improving their skills can work, no matter how much they may think the odds are against them at that moment. I began by telling them the following story about myself.

On the first day of my freshman year of high school, during gym class our teacher said we'd play a game of dodge ball. The basic rules were that two teams, ten on each side, would compete. Each team had to stay behind a line drawn down the middle of the gym. Two dodge balls (basically soccer balls) would be used. If you threw a ball and hit an opponent who couldn't catch the ball, he was out. If he caught the ball, you were out. Anyone holding one of the balls in their hands could use it to block a ball thrown at them. Pretty simple rules; now let the games begin.

I had played a lot of dodge ball in the school yards and streets of New York City and developed pretty good skills. I was ready for the action when the gym teacher blew the whistle. Balls started flying fast and furious. I can still hear the screeching of sneakers on the gym floor as both teams ran furiously cutting left, right, toward the line, away from the line, diving to catch balls and then throwing them as hard as possible toward an opponent, often at their legs and knees, making a catch difficult.

After about 15 minutes I had a problem. It was a major one. Everyone on my team was out. I was the only one left on our side of the line. This situation was complicated by the fact that no one on the other team had been eliminated. I was facing ten guys who were ready, and very eager, to take me out.

One opponent raced to the line and threw the ball low; I blocked it with the ball in my hands and returned a fast throw that hit him in the leg. He was out; nine to go. And so it went. Somehow I believed that as long as I remained standing and focused on one opportunity at a time, I had a chance. Before long I was in what athletes call "the zone." Everything seems to happen in slow motion and with great clarity. Before I knew it, the game was over, I had eliminated all ten opponents and I was being hoisted on the shoulders of my delirious team mates. It was a nice way to start high school.

But more important than the win was what I learned that day. You can trust that as long as you're still standing and trying and reaching to beat the odds, great things can happen. Drawing my story to a close, I looked many members of the audience in the eye and said they could trust in the program and in their ability not only to become a better public speaker, but maybe even a great one. Up to this point their past experience may suggest that the odds are stacked against them. "Not so," I said. "Trust me, you can do it. I did, not just on the gym floor that day but at the podium, practicing for many hours with the support and positive feedback of my fellow club members, which enabled me to continually improve."

This is who I am

The first question people ask themselves when they realize that you want to influence them is "who is this person?" Telling a story helps to communicate what you want them to know about you and how *you* would like them to perceive you. Rather than just telling them, demonstrating who you are with a story is a much more effective approach.

For example, imagine that you are in a group of people who are about to hear my presentation on improving your persuasive communication skills. I stand at the podium and face you and the rest of the audience. I gesture to my "this-is-who-I-am slide" on the screen behind me and basically recite a few facts: my name is Ken Neal, I have 20 years of experience marketing technology products, I have worked for X, Y and Z companies, I am a certified Electronic Content Management Practitioner, etc. At this point you may be thinking, "Here we have another expert about to give a straightforward, probably technical and boring presentation on how to communicate. Where is the nearest exit?"

However, rather than reciting my credentials by rote, suppose I take another approach. Suppose I open by relating a version of the "Sonic Jacket story" with which I opened this chapter. The story tells you who I am and what my presentation is about in a much different way. Within the story you learn that I've marketed technology products for leading companies over a span of 20 years. You experience how I used the persuasive techniques I've learned over the years to successfully launch a product. You laugh a bit at some of the humorous elements of the quirky product, how people related to it and how the publicity initiative achieved results far beyond what I anticipated. Maybe now you think, "This presenter has years of experience, seems not only committed to but actually enjoys using effective communication skills and has a sense of humor. This might not be boring. I might learn something interesting. Perhaps I'll stay in my seat."

Personal stories enable you to reveal aspects of yourself that remain hidden in a PowerPoint slide. They demonstrate who you are. And your "this-is-who-I-am story" doesn't necessarily have to be personal. There are countless fables, anecdotes, historical stories, stories told to you by friends and family, current event stories and parables you can adapt. Any of these can establish and express who you are if you believe in the story and tell it with your heart. As Annette Simmons explains:

> "When a person tells a story about Mother Teresa that reveals he understands gratitude and the humility of learning from others, we can conclude he is not bound by ego and can be trusted to listen to what we have to say. If the story he chooses to tell reveals that he understands self-sacrifice, we feel he can be trusted to blend compassion with desire for self gain. When we see through a story that someone has learned to recognize his own flaws and not hide in

denial, we assume he can be trusted to deal head-on with tough issues rather than pretend things are 'just fine'."

(Simmons, 2006)

This is why I am here

Once people have a sense of your trustworthiness and an idea of who you are there is still at least one more issue they want to be clear about: why are you here? If they are going to listen; to allow themselves to be influenced and cooperate with you, they need to know what's in it for you – *before* they know what's in it for them. This is a natural human need and if you ignore it you risk your persuasiveness.

Only emphasizing what your audience has to gain by listening to your message leaves you open to being considered insincere or seen as possibly hiding something. People will consider your pitches, ideas and proposals only if they are clear about your potential gains and they believe those gains to be reasonable, representing healthy ambitions and desires. Being selfish is alright if you are upfront about it; then your audience is ready to hear what's also in it for them. This is the value of a "why I am here" story. It reveals enough for people to distinguish between your healthy self-interest and possible exploitation.

For example, if you are on an altruistic mission you need to start with a story that provides evidence of that. Don't assume that your audience automatically buys into your altruism. You need to highlight why you quit your corporate job that paid $100,000 to teach art to young students at a fraction of your former salary. You need to tell that story if you want to interest students and their parents in your program.

On the other hand, you might be on a sales mission. Before you launch into your proposal spotlighting why your technology solution could work for your prospect (what's in it for them), tell the company executives upfront that you want their business. You believe (sincerely) that they are the kind of company you want to work with and by helping them meet their challenges and achieve successful results your company thrives as well. In fact you may, like many technology providers today, state that you're building financial incentives into your proposal. If your company meets or exceeds objectives that the prospect agrees to, such as reducing costs by a specified amount, then your company gets a bonus. Both sides win. Why not briefly tell that story upfront then offer the details on how your solution will reduce costs and streamline the prospect's operations?

No matter how many times it's been said, executives like to hear that you want their business. Then, with your goal established, they're more open to listening about how your solution just might achieve the results they need.

Up to this point we've explored how two key factors – creating an emotional experience through dramatic product demonstrations, creative visuals and expressing emotions and telling a story that has meaning to your audience – can take your persuasive skills to a much higher level. One additional factor, however, can be the difference between competent and very good, between very good and excellent, between excellent and great. It's a characteristic demonstrated by many of the leaders, thinkers and successful business executives I've spotlighted so far. Lincoln had it. John D. Rockefeller had it. Steve Jobs had it. That characteristic is confidence. Let's look at the third element of mastering persuasiveness: the confidence factor.

The confidence factor

All of the keys to persuasiveness I've highlighted up to this point won't mean much if you're paralyzed with fear or just plain ineffective when presenting to your boss, your department, senior management or industry groups. Recall the story I related in the introduction of the records manager who convinced his boss that the company needed to spend thousands of dollars to create a recordkeeping program that would protect the company against superfund lawsuits. Imagine the records manager trying to achieve his objective without the ability to speak with confidence.

Yet fear of public speaking, ranging from mild discomfort to sheer terror, is precisely the obstacle that many business professionals face. In a standup routine at the end of a "Seinfeld" episode, comedian Jerry Seinfeld expressed it this way: "According to most studies, people's number one fear is public speaking. Number two is death. Death is number two. Does that seem right? That means to the average person, if you have to go to a funeral, you're better off in the casket than doing the eulogy."

The good news is that there's an alternative to wishing you were in the coffin. There's a relatively straightforward way to learn to speak with confidence, though it takes time. When you combine being more at ease in front of people with the other two persuasive factors I highlighted, your communications effectiveness can skyrocket.

Why are so many of us uncomfortable speaking in front of people? The key reason is that we never get enough practice. Unless you were born with innate public-speaking talent (which wouldn't correlate with success anyway as we'll see shortly), or you have a career that demands you constantly present in front of groups, you never get enough opportunity to become more comfortable, increase your skills or both. Presenting to senior management once or twice a year during the national business meeting or occasionally at a quarterly review session will never give you the chance to advance your skills. And if you're among the many who dread the experience; the occasional presentation is not going to cure what ails you. Only one thing will: practice. And it needs to be a specific form of practice. But first, if you believe that some people just have an innate talent for public speaking and that's the secret to their success, let's dispel that myth right now.

What really creates expertise?

It's easy to believe, especially if you avoid public speaking at all costs, that other confident, successful presenters like Steve Jobs were born with a natural ability that drives their success on stage. On the contrary, extensive research indicates talent has virtually nothing to do with it. What does? The *Harvard Business Review* lets us in on the secret.

"Back in 1985, Benjamin Bloom, a professor of education at the University of Chicago, published a landmark book, *Developing Talent in Young People*, which examined the critical factors that contribute to talent. He took a deep retrospective look at the childhoods of 120 elite performers who had won international competitions or awards in fields ranging from music and the arts to mathematics and neurology. Surprisingly, Bloom's work found no early indicators that could have predicted the virtuosos' success. Subsequent research indicating that there is no correlation between IQ and expert performance in fields such as chess, music, sports and medicine has borne out his findings. The only innate differences that turn out to be significant – and they matter primarily in sports – are height and body size.

So what does correlate with success? One thing emerges very clearly from Bloom's work: All the superb performers he investigated had practiced intensively, had studied with devoted teachers, and been supported enthusiastically by their families throughout their developing years. Later research building on Bloom's pioneering study revealed that the amount and quality of practice were key factors in the level of expertise people achieved. Consistently and overwhelmingly, the evidence showed that experts are always made, not born."

(Ericsson et al., 2007)

What exactly is an expert?

So it's not innate talent, but practice, that can help you not only become a more competent and accomplished communicator and presenter, but a proven authority in records and IT management as well. However, there are two caveats to consider as you embark on the road to superior performance. One is that you must engage in a specific form of practice, referred to as "deliberate practice;" the second is that achieving confidence and true expertise takes time. I'll highlight these two considerations in a moment, but first let's examine exactly what I mean by an "expert" because being clear about what constitutes real expertise will help you create and implement an improvement plan that works.

The *Harvard Business Review* article asserts that you are a true expert if you can pass three tests. First, you must be able to achieve concrete results that are consistently superior to those of your peers.

Second, you must produce concrete results. A tennis player, for example, must win matches in sanctioned tournaments. Accredited world-class public speakers often win competitions (such as the Toastmasters World Championship of Public Speaking) and are consistently invited to speak at premier events.

Third, your performance must be able to be replicated and measured. As the British scientist Lord Kelvin stated, "If you cannot measure it, you cannot improve it." It's impossible to improve your speed in the 100-yard dash without timing your performance. You need to know how fast you are right now, tomorrow and the next day in order to continually make adjustments that will significantly improve your speed over time.

These tests are easier to quantify in some fields, particularly sports. In competitions the playing field is even; everyone is judged by the same rules. You know who jumped the highest, who ran the fastest time and who came in first. An even playing field permits comparisons among individuals over time, which can also be applied to business. Retailers, for example, run competitions among store managers to identify which store had the highest profitability.

Table 6.1   Elements to consider about expertise

Element	Insight
Accounts of expertise are not always reliable	Anecdotes and second-hand accounts of events often provide notoriously unreliable examples of true expertise. One reason is that these accounts are filtered through individual biases, experience or lack of it and plain faulty memory. Recounting a story is not the same as solid research
Experts can be wrong, and often are	Remember that a hallmark of expertise is producing measurable, consistently superior performance. In 1976 French wine experts argued that French wines were superior to California wines. A blind taste test proved them wrong when California wines received higher scores. They continued to argue that California reds in particular would never age as well as the famous French reds. A blind taste test in 2006 proved them wrong again
Gut feelings can be wrong, and often are	It is tempting to follow a common belief that the best way to improve your performance is to relax and follow your intuition. Listening to your "gut feelings" is a popular concept and occasionally can be valuable in routine situations. Informed intuition, however, is the result of deliberate practice. You can't consistently improve your ability to make good management decisions, for example, without considerable practice, careful consideration of the results and analysis of why you made a good or bad decision
You don't need a new tennis racquet	Just as it's tempting to just relax and follow your instincts, it's an attractive idea that you can improve your management performance by adopting new and better methods. This is similar to a tennis player believing that he can improve his game by using a new racquet. Being a tennis player myself and having tried many new racquets over the years, I learned that nothing substitutes for consistent, carefully controlled practice

Adapted from Ericsson et al. (2007)

In creating your own plan for improving your presentation skills, Table 6.1 offers some elements to keep in mind when judging expertise.

Are you ready for deliberate practice?

Now that we have a clearer picture of what constitutes expertise, let's examine two key ways you can consistently become more confident in front of an audience and eventually evolve into a master of persuasive communication. Earlier I referred to a specific type of practice, "deliberate practice." This is key number one.

Not all practice makes perfect. It takes a deliberate form of practice to approach mastery. Most people practice on skills they already have, what they already know. Deliberate practice is different. It focuses on consistently practicing what you're not good at, what you may not even know at all. Research has shown that this is the only form of practice that enables you to become initially more comfortable and then evolve to eventually achieve confidence, competence and expertise.

Tennis anyone?

To illustrate this point, let's imagine you are learning to play tennis for the first time. In the early phases you might read books, watch videos and take some lessons as you try to understand the basics of different strokes such as the serve, backhand and drop shot as well as the intricacies of footwork, when and how to approach the net and more. You put in a lot practice with novices on your level and play as often as possible. In a surprisingly short time (possibly around 50 hours), you develop some skills and your game evolves. (I once took three hours of lessons at a Club Med – my introduction to tennis. Having played racquetball and squash for years, I then determined I was ready to enter the club's tennis tournament. Not surprisingly, I didn't win. That's called overconfidence. I had many more hours of deliberate practice to undergo before my game was truly competitive. However, those first three hours instilled in me a love of the game.)

After a period of time spent practicing and playing, your shots, strategy and overall game start to become automatic. You think less and play more from instinct. You're fairly confident that your game is solid and tennis starts to become a social event in which you occasionally concentrate on a particular shot or strategy. Your skill has leveled off and no matter how much you play might remain at this level for decades.

Why does this happen? Because in a social game of tennis you don't have the opportunity to, for example, improve your first serve. This would require serving a number of times from the same position, getting feedback on your toss, grip, racquet position, etc. and then making adjustments to correct your mistakes. This enables you to get better. Pros in tennis and golf take multiple shots from the same position when they train and when they check out a tennis court or golf course before a tournament.

From tennis to records management

This kind of deliberate practice can be adapted to develop business and leadership skills. The classic example is the mock case history method taught in business schools and used by many companies in their training classes. I once took a records management training class focused on how to work with a current or prospective client so you can determine ways to help improve their program. For several hours we covered assessing a current records program, how to leverage the benefits of document imaging, when to update retention schedules, how to implement an effective archiving system and much more.

After a half day of study and discussion, I thought we were done. Not so. Our next task was to read a mock case study based on a real life client situation and create a recommended program that would help improve the company's records program. Our programs would be analyzed by the teachers and we would receive instant feedback that would enable us to improve the decisions and recommendations we made. This in turn would enhance our ability to handle actual client situations.

Deliberate practice in public speaking

Let's examine how deliberate practice might work for improving your management presentation and general public-speaking skills. My model is based on my years of experience participating in Toastmasters International.[4] It's a non-profit organization and I don't receive any benefit for promoting the organization. I have heard good things about many other organizations, such as Dale Carnegie, and individuals who do a great job of helping people advance their skills. Toastmasters is the one

I am familiar with, having gone through its training programs for over ten years, including achieving an Advanced Toastmaster certification and stretching my abilities by entering Toastmaster-sanctioned public-speaking competitions.

The Toastmaster program is a great example of how to apply deliberate practice to public speaking. The initial approach, when I went through the training, includes a manual that outlines ten critical elements of public speaking such as using vocal variety, storytelling and body language to build confidence and increase persuasiveness. The basic program provides the opportunity to give a speech on each skill when you feel ready. Your speech is timed, someone in the group is responsible for counting "mistakes" such the number of "ahs" and "ums" you make instead of pausing, and you receive immediate feedback from an evaluator so that you can improve the skill you're practicing or move on to the next skill.

Additionally, a part of each meeting is devoted to extemporaneous speaking. You are given a question and have up to two minutes to provide your answer in front of the group (called "table topics"). All of these activities are done in a very supportive environment; some clubs give trophies or ribbons for the best speech and table topics answer of the meeting. There is often plenty of good humor to go around and excellent feedback is provided by, in my experience, great people who have the same goal as you.

A personal best

I started participating in a local Toastmasters club because, limited to speaking in front of groups at business meetings once or twice a year, I never had enough opportunity to feel comfortable and improve my presentation skills. I believed that I wasn't very persuasive, would never be completely comfortable in front of an audience and couldn't possibly enjoy public speaking. I didn't know it then, but I was wrong on all counts. The Toastmasters program gave me the opportunity to craft speeches on topics that were personally meaningful to me. The specific feedback I received helped me quickly develop a comfort level and a competence I lacked up to that point. My speeches improved both in content and delivery as I became more effective at using vocal inflections, telling stories and incorporating humor into my presentations. Most importantly, I learned how to use body language and movement in a way that both discharged nervousness and increased my effectiveness in delivering a message. Within a few months after starting the program, I won my first trophy for best speech at one of the meetings. That was a personal best I couldn't have imagined.

A short time later another personal breakthrough occurred. I was hired as public relations manager for a major technology consulting and services company. A few weeks into the job my division scheduled a meeting in which I and five of my colleagues were to introduce ourselves and deliver a 20-minute presentation with PowerPoint slides outlining our communications strategy and recommendations for the next quarter. The presentations would take place in an auditorium with about 50 people in attendance including the company's senior management.

A prescription for anxiety

For me, normally this situation would be a prescription for major anxiety. But this time things were different. Following the principles that I practiced at my Toastmasters meetings, I wrote what I felt confident was a well-organized presentation. Each slide was brief, including only a few bullet points, and the overall presentation was structured to deliver three key messages. I would incorporate a brief story and make some humorous observations during my talk. As I sat waiting for my introduction, I hoped it would all come together. My name was called.

Standing in front of the group I did something I never did before at high-pressured business meetings. Instead of intently focusing on my slides and basically reading them, I barely looked at them. I looked at my audience. Instead of standing still, I moved around, discharging nervous energy and using body language to emphasize points and concepts that I thought were important. I used vocal variety to more effectively deliver my story and share a few humorous comments. Twenty minutes went by like twenty seconds. To my amazement, I felt confident and actually enjoyed giving the presentation. Another personal breakthrough had just occurred.

During the years since that moment I have had exciting opportunities to give presentations. The largest was to a group of over 200 records managers at an annual conference. I had a stage with a sound system and a huge screen that made my PowerPoint slides look like an IMAX movie. But whether a presentation will involve 10 or 200 people, I always practice diligently before each event, rereading, vocalizing and sometimes even acting out the material. The value of practice, and my Toastmasters training, will always be with me.

The only way

Whether you are just beginning to improve your presentation skills or have years of experience under your belt, it's helpful to remember that great speakers are not born; they earn their skill the hard way, the only way; by working at it. One of the speakers I admire is Winston Churchill. Here is an interesting insight into his development as a public speaker as well as advice he offers that all aspiring communicators should memorize.

"Winston Churchill is one of the most revered leaders in history. As the prime minister of Great Britain during World War II, he inspired the nation and the world with his passionate, compelling speeches. He was certainly one of the most influential persons in British history, and his speeches are consistently ranked as the best ever given. Paul Johnson, a Churchill scholar, writes in *Churchill*, 'no man did more to preserve freedom and democracy and the values we hold dear in the West.' Here are a few lessons we can learn from Churchill's magnificent oratory skills.

First, and perhaps most importantly, it's possible to become a great speaker even if you're not a natural at public speaking. Churchill himself was not born a great orator. In fact, he had a slight stammer and lisp when he was young. He spent hours and hours crafting his speeches, practicing and perfecting each word. His good friend Lord Birkenhead said, 'Winston has spent the best years of his life writing impromptu speeches.' He put in countless hours of work making his speeches flawless to incite inspiration in a desperate audience. His dedicated effort obviously made a difference to millions in an extremely trying time.

You don't have to be a natural at presenting to be successful at it. Even one of the greatest orators of the twentieth century had to practice, practice and practice to perfect the craft. 'Continuous effort not strength or intelligence is the key to unlocking our potential,' Churchill said. Keep practicing and perfecting your presentation and your effort will pay off in the end."[5]

Bringing the six key skills to life

There is no ultimate formula for persuasiveness and there is no endpoint to improving your skill in this area; it is a lifelong commitment. But, as Churchill instructs us, keep practicing and your dedication will pay off. My suggestion is that by continually and deliberately practicing the three elements I've highlighted in this chapter – the experience factor, the story factor and the confidence factor – you'll always be on solid ground in your journey toward becoming an effective communicator. You may also discover at some point, as I did early in my Toastmasters training, that you've developed your own voice and your own style; that you've evolved from reluctant presenter to actually enjoying the challenge of crafting and delivering a message you feel passionately about. That kind of enjoyment can be very satisfying, and exhilarating.

The six communications skills I've highlighted are not abstract or theoretical. They are put into action every day as recordkeeping professionals, IT managers and other business executives fight for their programs and ideas, adjust when they encounter obstacles and delays, and persist until they win or decide to live and fight another day. In one of the case history examples I'll highlight in the next chapter, a records management executive worked for over two years to get an industry association program adopted. Her commitment to the program backed by her communications skills eventually won the day. Let's bring our six key skills to life by hearing her story.

Notes

1. Retrieved 28 September 2013 from *http://en.wikipedia.org/wiki/Albert_Mehrabian*
2. The iPhone launch presentation is available at *http://www.youtube.com/watch?v=t2MOwQ089eQ*; for the Stanford commencement speech visit *http://www.youtube.com/watch?v=UF8uR6Z6KLc*
3. Osteen adapted the story from Waitley (1995).
4. To learn more about Toastmasters International visit *www.toastmasters.org*
5. *Presentation Lessons from Winston Churchill*. Retrieved 14 October 2013 from *www.ethos3.com/2012/03/presentation-lessons-from-winston-churchill/*

7

Case histories: why should you adopt my business case?

"If records and information managers don't have communications skills to stand their ground and persuasively argue for their programs, other departments will win the competition for budget."

(Cheryl, Certified Records Manager)

Abstract: An important practical application of the six key communication skills is the business case. It is a critical document for records and information managers who want to successfully compete for budget and obtain support for their programs. This chapter highlights two case histories in which records and information management professionals used the six key communication skills to research, draft and present a business case that was successfully adopted. One case involves the story of an association president who campaigned to have the executive board approve and publish a set of records management principles and best practices. The other case focuses on a records management expert for a managed services provider who competed for and won a project to implement a records program for the human resources department of a technology company.

Key words: Association of Records Managers & Administrators, The Principles of records management, GAAP, business case, records management accountability, Information Governance Maturity Model, effective PowerPoint presentation, persuasive presentation, the six key communication skills, HR records, personnel records, HR recordkeeping, HR records auditing, HR records compliance, records management risk reduction, records management disaster recovery, records imaging.

I pointed out in the Introduction that one of the most practical applications of the six key communication skills for records and information managers is the business case. It is a critical document for records and information managers who want to win support and funding for their programs.

Cheryl, a certified records manager with over 20 years of experience helping organizations launch and improve their records management programs, agrees. She says that "Knowing how to write and effectively present a business case is important because records managers have a budget. They have to defend that budget and periodically convince senior management to expand it. If they don't have the communications skills to persuasively argue their case, they won't get the funding they need. Remember, many enterprises allocate budget based on how well different departments argue for their portion of the pie."

Competing for a slice of the pie

Cheryl points out that records and IT management departments often compete with each other for budget. In the late 1990s IT departments were receiving a good portion of budget dollars. Why? Because one of their arguments was based on the need to comply with Sarbanes Oxley and other industry regulations, which was and still is an important issue. As IT departments were deploying systems to comply with the regulations, they increasingly had to call on records managers to help organize and preserve vital records. Despite the growing role of records management in helping the organization improve compliance, the IT department continued to get increased budgets. Funding for many records management departments remained stagnant; the recordkeeping function was not getting its share of the pie. Records managers soon realized what was happening but at that time, according to Cheryl, they weren't able to effectively argue their case. A key reason was that historically records managers simply accepted the budgets they were allocated. They didn't have the experience to craft successful business cases and the communications skills to defend them. Consequently, they didn't have the ear of upper management. This situation is changing.

The story of "The Principles"

Cheryl has been an active member for many years of ARMA (Association of Records Managers and Administrators), the leading industry association for records managers with over 27,000 members around the world.[1] She had the opportunity to closely watch how a past ARMA president used her strategic communication skills, credibility and persistence to drive the adoption of a major program that has helped elevate records management as a profession.

Because the president's goal was to improve the perception of records management as a profession and help establish it as a vital corporate function, she began by investigating programs, credentials and guidelines adopted by other professions. One set of practices stood out: the Generally Accepted Accounting Principles (GAAP), a common set of accounting principles, standards and procedures that companies use to compile their financial statements. GAAP are a combination of authoritative standards (set by policy boards) and the commonly accepted ways of recording and reporting accounting information. The structure of GAAP enables accountants, and others, basically to know what accountants do and it helps clarify the value they provide. Similar standards were precisely what ARMA and the records management profession needed. The concept of "The Principles" was born.

Cheryl explains that the president started by drafting eight principles that would be the foundation of the business case. The principles would define requirements for a document being considered a "record" and specify criteria for an effective records management program. An example of the latter is the principle of accountability, which states that a senior executive should oversee the company's information governance program and delegate responsibility for records and information management to appropriate individuals.

Using key communication skills

The president knew that using the communication skills we've examined so far was critical to success. She was aware that, in order to persuade the ARMA executive board to adopt the initiative, the eight principles needed to be brief, clear and direct so that organizational management could easily understand them and records managers could implement them efficiently and relatively quickly. She also knew that in order to be successful, from a communications perspective, she needed to take a strategic approach and establish credibility for herself and the business case.

Her strategic approach consisted of two main phases: build widespread acceptance of the program at the grassroots level – ARMA chapters located throughout the country – then present the business case and document summarizing The Principles for approval by the association's executive board.

She began by gathering volunteers (including Cheryl) who provided feedback on the initiative and helped create an initial one-page document summarizing The Principles. The volunteers and the ARMA president then scheduled as many meetings as possible with the chapters to explain the document, the strategy behind it and why it would motivate organizations to take records managers and their programs more seriously. Because the original document was brief, clear and easy to understand, enthusiasm for it began to build. The chapters became excited about the association's new direction and started putting some of The Principles in action. Many records managers began seeing an increased appreciation for their programs. They were being invited to the executive table.

Asking questions and listening pays off

The association president also focused on asking numerous questions and intently listening, which revealed one key criterion that had to be met in order for The Principles to be adopted. The overall program needed to be measurable. Records managers and their company's senior management needed a "scale" that would help records managers and their companies see a clear picture of what effective information governance looks like. This scale would eventually become the ARMA Information Governance Maturity Model, based on the eight principles as well as industry standards, best practices and legal/regulatory requirements. The Principles and the Maturity Model would function together. The former states the hallmarks of effective governance; the latter goes beyond a mere statement to define the characteristics of various levels of recordkeeping programs – a gauge by which organizations could assess their current records program. Asking questions and listening paid off: the concept of the Maturity Model would eventually be a key factor in getting The Principles approved.

After many months, the first phase of the president's strategy was complete. Extensive feedback was obtained and incorporated into the program. Ideas were tested and refined. The program's credibility was established and growing. Many of the ARMA chapters were putting The Principles into action and getting positive business benefits. What better strategy than to propose a program that was already succeeding, already had a measurement system created and was already credible with association members at local chapters across the country?

It seemed that virtually everyone at the local level knew about the program and its value. They had provided ideas; helped analyze, refine and test The Principles and the Maturity Model by incorporating them into their recordkeeping programs and getting results. Now it was time for the ARMA president to get the buy-in of the executive board.

Never letting go

Launching the second phase of her strategy, the association president began by ensuring that The Principles initiative was highlighted at ARMA executive board meetings, which were scheduled every three months. Once she started that process, she never let go until the program was approved. She continually listened, incorporated feedback into her next presentation, stayed confident and maintained momentum for the program's approval. Her initial research and program proposals as well as her presentations at the local chapter and executive board levels spanned over three years. Toward the end of the process The Principles were formally announced during an October meeting and would be published the following January. By this point the document stating The Principles was ten pages; long enough to be taken seriously by senior leadership at any organization but still brief enough to be easily understood and put into action. The Information Governance Maturity Model "grading" document that would enable companies to make basic assessments about their current records program was eight pages. Like The Principles, it was substantial yet concise enough to be actionable.

Presenting to the board

I asked Cheryl, who attended one of the president's final presentations to the executive board before The Principles were adopted, to describe the session. I was particularly interested in how the president communicated her business case. According to Cheryl there were about 40 people in the room. The president, planning to keep her presentation within 30 minutes, stood at a podium with a screen for displaying PowerPoint slides behind her. One interesting detail: the president was professionally dressed in a tailored business suit. Cheryl explains that this element stood out because it is acceptable for records managers, like many other IT professionals such as programmers, to dress informally. The association president obviously wanted everything that day, including her appearance, to underscore the credibility of her initiative.

Another interesting detail: while she would be addressing her audience for about half an hour, the president only had *five PowerPoint slides* to display. And the slides had minimal content, mostly images and graphics that told the story of The Principles up to that point – how the local chapters helped refine and test the program, the business results they achieved and demographic information on the program participants to date. The latter data were provided to emphasize the point that the grassroots initiative involved records managers from companies of all sizes across a diverse range of industries. The Principles weren't relevant to only one type of enterprise; they could benefit virtually any organization that wanted to implement and maintain an effective recordkeeping program.

Being strategic and persuasive

What made the president's strategic approach to the presentation a good one? For one, she knew her audience according to Cheryl. All of the board members were volunteers. The demands of their business and personal lives were many, so the president kept her presentation relatively brief. Second, the president tailored her business case to the interests and needs of the board and the association. From the moment she began to speak, no one in the audience needed to wonder, "What's in it for me?" That question was addressed and several possible objections anticipated by quickly communicating three key messages: (1) we need to elevate the professionalism of the records management function; (2) if we don't, our jobs will remain stagnant and lack the security and salary they deserve and (3) adopting The Principles and associated Information Governance Maturity Model is the best way to address the first two issues.

As Cheryl recalls, besides being grounded in a solid strategy, the president's delivery was persuasive. She was well rehearsed but never read from any of the slides. Perhaps most importantly, she let her feelings show. She was passionate about the program, believed in it, had fought long and hard for it, and wasn't about to hold back her enthusiasm at that moment. The Principles were formally adopted and published four months later. Case closed. (Or more appropriately, *business case* closed.)

Before turning to our next case history example, Table 7.1 highlights tactical ways the association president applied the six key communication skills in different ways and at different times during her three-year campaign to get The Principles adopted. Keep in mind that many tactics span several or all of the six skills.

The story of The Principles illustrates a case where a business professional used the six communication skills to sell a program at the

Table 7.1   Campaigning for The Principles

Communication skill	Tactics
Be brief	Drafted original document was only one page; final approved document was still concise at only ten pages; presentation to the executive board comprised only five slides; presentation slides contained mostly graphics and minimal written content; board presentation was contained to within 30 minutes
Be clear	Language describing The Principles was clearly stated and could be easily understood by records professionals or any organizational executive; presentation to the executive board focused on only three key messages
Be receptive	Consistently asked questions and incorporated feedback into revised program proposals; based on feedback the associated Maturity Model was created to ensure that programs applying The Principles could be benchmarked and improvement activities could be measured
Be strategic	Based the original concept on GAAP, an accepted accounting industry standard; gained initial local chapter involvement and acceptance of the program; tailored the three key messages to the main concerns of the executive board and other association members
Be credible	Tested the program at local chapters; presented data on how the program was already succeeding; displayed a polished, professional appearance; offered demographic information establishing the program's relevance to all organizations, despite size or industry
Be persuasive	Showed passion for the program during the executive board presentation; was rehearsed but did not read from slides; knew her audience; knew her "stuff"

industry association level. Now let's turn to an example that involves selling to a prospective client. This is the story of Marissa, a director of records management for a major business process outsourcing (BPO) services provider, who sold and implemented a comprehensive records program to the human resources (HR) division of a leading technology company. An interesting element of this story: Marissa and her team won the business despite initially having no experience in human resources. Communication skills and professionalism made all the difference.

The story of "the paper chase"

Kristine, the chief human resources officer for a leading technology outsourcing company, felt that her department was always chasing paper, and people. Most of the company's 5000 employees worked at client sites located throughout the U.S., Canada and the Philippines. When Kristine's HR team at headquarters needed to retrieve a document pertaining to one of the company's many regional offices, a staffer had to go through files, find the paper document and then scan and email it or ship it by postal mail. Since most of the employees at the regional offices are dedicated to maintaining on-site client service, often no one was standing by to handle clerical requests. Thus, the simple act of accessing a document could end up taking one or more days. And in many cases, a single employee's records were scattered about multiple office locations, especially if the employee had relocated during his or her employment.

The chief human resources officer knew that the situation needed to be fixed. At the very least, paper documents needed to be transformed into digital files so they could be stored in a centralized database and retrieved more quickly. To find a services provider that could do the job, Kristine began by issuing a "request for information" document. A number of prospects responded. Kristine eventually narrowed the field to three companies. She invited them to research, draft and present a proposal to Andrea and other company executives. One of the companies invited was Marissa's BPO services firm.

A credibility challenge

Despite being a records management expert with years of experience creating programs for well-known companies across a range of industries, Marissa knew that she had a credibility challenge to overcome if she was going to win the business. "At the beginning of the proposal phase, Kristine asked where we had implemented records programs for HR departments," Marissa says. "The answer was nowhere. So I knew that during the proposal process and for the presentation we had to work hard and fast to establish credibility in HR processes." As I outlined in Chapter 5, one of the actions you can take if you're not competent in a given area is to become competent. That's exactly what Marissa did.

She began by asking the right questions, listening and learning important details about Kristine's company and the HR records management challenges they faced. The proposal research process for all three firms competing for the business took about six weeks. During that time Marissa became proficient enough in the technology company's HR processes that she could speak to Kristine and her team in their language, not as Marissa describes it, "records management speak."

The interview strategy

One of the strategies Marissa used to quickly become competent in the company's HR operations was to interview executives who managed major areas within the HR division, such as employee benefits and training. This approach enabled Marissa to achieve an in-depth understanding of the different document types, the workflows associated with them and how long the company was legally required to retain each document type. Marissa increasingly gained a clear picture of the company's regulatory compliance needs, internal and external audit requirements and other issues that Kristine's staff had to grapple with daily.

After a few weeks Marissa began discussing the HR department's challenges with Kristine in the same language Kristine would use. Marissa understood that auditing was a big challenge. She could explain why the company's current paper-based system was compromising its ability to confirm that it had every appropriate document for every employee. This was a critical issue. Each employee had over 40 HR-related documents associated with them. The technology company needed to ensure that it had all of those 60 documents in order to respond to requests from federal and local government agencies.

Marissa could also explain why disaster preparedness was another key issue for the HR department. Fire, flood and natural decay are the enemies of paper-based records. In addition to causing operational problems, Marissa emphasized that these forces put the technology company at risk since some of the employee documents were legally required to be retained for decades. Many organizations, like the technology company, have no plan for disaster and decay.

By the end of the proposal phase, Marissa could describe with confidence the company's challenges and what was needed to meet each one, from audits to industry compliance to disaster recovery plans. By the time Marissa was scheduled to present her proposal, she had Kristine thinking differently. Originally Kristine thought she simply needed a document-scanning solution. "Now she wasn't even thinking in records management terms," Marissa notes. "She's thinking in terms of 'I need a solution that just works for my department and its special challenges'." That's precisely the solution Marissa and her team planned to propose.

The presentation

Each competing firm had two hours to present their proposal. Marissa's presentation had only 15 slides. She and her team planned to spend most of their time engaging the audience in a discussion. Her approach included something different; something that distinguished her presentation from the competitors. She brought in the HR executives she had interviewed during her research process. "I wanted to state my findings in front of them," Marissa explains. "This would give them a chance to agree with, correct or dispute my insights. Agreements would enhance the credibility of my proposal; corrections or objections would give me the opportunity to respond and adapt my proposal on the spot."

From the beginning of her presentation Marissa had everyone in the room working as one team. It was clear to her audience that Marissa had listened to them. She described the technology company's current document and records management workflows, pinpointed problems within each workflow that needed to be fixed and detailed how she and her team would fix them including timelines and costs. "We clarified gaps in the company's current records program and stated how our team would fill those gaps," Marissa says. To support her case, she shared quotes and statistics provided by the executives during her interviews. Her presentation communicated a key message: "You started with one idea, let's digitize our records. We'll do that and more, enabling you to meet other critical needs that will vastly improve your program." The latter includes creating a records retention schedule, classification scheme and document repository. With Marissa's comprehensive solution, HR records would be compliant, secure and could be accessed quickly when needed.

Winning the business; getting to work

Marissa's team won the business; then they got to work. During the next eight months they digitized records for 12,000 current and past employees dating back five years. At an average of 40 documents per employee, this totals close to 500,000 images.

The initiative yielded a host of financial and operational benefits. Projected savings from the project will be approximately $200,000 over five years. Additionally, the HR records became digital records, rendering the original paper documents "copies" that can be destroyed as dictated by the company record retention schedule and policy.

For the technology company, now the physical location of a personnel record is irrelevant. A record is simply in the repository and any authorized HR employee with a web browser can retrieve any document at any time. Marissa's solution had put an end to the company's paper chase.

What better way to end the story

I asked Marissa for a few key takeaways for records managers. "My suggestion for records managers is to treat executives within their organization as clients," Marissa says. "Many records managers legitimately complain that senior executives don't take the recordkeeping function seriously. Of course they don't; it's not as important to them. Make it important by understanding their concerns, describing those concerns and solutions to their problems in the language they would use. If appropriate, give them a formal proposal."

Marissa also emphasized flexibility and learning. "Don't go to a meeting with one idea about how to fix a problem. With the technology company, my team had to continually revise our proposal every time we received significant new feedback. Besides being flexible, records and information managers have to stay current with industry trends, constantly researching and learning new approaches. A solution you implemented five years ago is probably not relevant today."

Marissa's final point was that as a records or information manager, if you want to shine then deliver everything you promise – and more. "Being aggressive about meeting deadlines is one way you maintain your credibility and enhance your reputation," she counsels. "We took this approach with the technology company and it paid dividends for our client and for us."

Marissa's approach did indeed pay off in one interesting respect. Kristine became a strong advocate of records management and Marissa's firm. In fact, Kristine now periodically joins Marissa on her sales presentations to talk about the positive impact Marissa's solution

Table 7.2   Ending the paper chase

Communication skill	Tactics
Be brief	Presentation had only 15 slides
Be clear	Did not use technical records management language but spoke to client in HR language; communicated one key message during presentation: you need more and we will do more
Be receptive	Continually asked questions, listened and adjusted; during the presentation, made proposal modifications on the spot in response to feedback
Be strategic	Interviewed HR department executives; encouraged both sides to act as a team during the presentation
Be credible	Became competent in HR by researching and studying the client; during the presentation, defined problems, solutions, timelines and costs to fix each problem
Be persuasive	Communicated gaps and needs beyond what the client had considered; included department executives at the presentation

had on her department. As Marissa describes it, "Kristine still doesn't really know what we do for a living; she just knows the solid benefits we provided. She knows that it worked for her. Often when we're talking to a prospect, Kristine is there helping us sell our proposal. You can't get a better ending to the story than that."

As we did with the story of The Principles, let's look at a summary of how Marissa's approach utilized each of the six communication skills in Table 7.2. As with the previous summary, most of the tactics apply to more than one skill.

Note

1. For more information on ARMA, The Principles, the Information Governance Maturity Model and recordkeeping best practices visit *www.arma.org*

Conclusion: communicate as well as you can

"Communication is a skill that you can learn. It's like riding a bicycle or typing. If you're willing to work at it, you can rapidly improve the quality of every part of your life."

(Brian Tracy)

The list of demands on our time and energy is long. You might wonder, "Do I really need to add to that list by trying to improve my communication skills?" I believe the answer is yes. One reason is that communicating as well as you can becomes its own reward. That may not seem evident in the beginning. It is work to read books, attend classes, study, submit writing samples and edit your text in an effort to improve your skills. It is work to find and join a public-speaking group, attend meetings, write speeches, get up in front of a group and present while trying to keep anxiety at bay; then gather feedback, adjust your approach and come back to speak another day.

However, in my experience, something may happen to you along the way. You realize you are improving. You start to enjoy communicating about topics and issues you care about. You begin looking forward to the challenge of trying to sell an idea to a group of senior executives. You may even become passionate about communicating well.

My passion for communicating

My passion for communicating began with my father, an actor who loved his job. It didn't matter what form it took. Performing in a television commercial was as important and valuable as appearing in a play, industry training film or movie. Acting to him was communication and throughout his life he challenged himself to continually improve because he enjoyed it and because improvement was its own reward.

He loved movies and he loved Shakespeare. When I was in grade school he took me to see Laurence Olivier in *Othello*. I had never seen anything like it on the big screen. I didn't understand most of the language yet it spoke to me in larger-than-life displays of love, jealously, rage, betrayal and death. I suddenly understood the power of language, the power of the image and the power of storytelling. In eighth grade I entered my first public-speaking contest. With the help of my parents I wrote a speech about the Statue of Liberty. It was titled "Meet Miss Liberty" and contained interesting facts and stories about one of America's most iconic national monuments. I would close the speech by reciting Emma Lazarus' famous poem, *The New Colossus*, inscribed on a tablet within the pedestal upon which the statue stands. My speech was a good one because, with the help of my father, it incorporated all the six key communication skills although I didn't know anything about them at the time.

I remember sitting in my chair, waiting, looking anxiously out at the audience. The eyes of fellow students, parents and judges looked back at me. When it was my turn to speak, I took a deep breath, stood in front of my audience, and invited my audience to meet Miss Liberty. I started a bit shaky but got better as the speech progressed. Toward the end, noticing my father in the back row, I realized it was with his voice I was speaking. It was his love of communication and presentation continuing through me. I was awarded the second-place prize, which was nice but not what really mattered. I had made a breakthrough.

It stays with you

Which brings me to my second point: you should continue to communicate as well as you can because every breakthrough you make stays with you forever. In the quote I cite at the beginning of this chapter, author Brian Tracy aptly compares learning communication skills to riding a bicycle or typing. Once you learn these skills, you always have them. Every breakthrough you make in improving your bike riding, whether moving from a 5-speed to a 10-speed or entering competitive races, is yours for the rest of your life.

It was years before I stood in front of an audience again. In college a teacher recognized my enthusiasm for literature. To encourage my passion and good grades, she gave me a gift. In lieu of a final test for my course grade, I could instead decide on a project and confer with her during its development and completion. We would decide on my grade together.

My project was to read as many Aldous Huxley books as possible during the semester – I had read one of his books and became an instant fan – and then create and teach a class about Huxley's life, his books and share their impact on me with the students. Midway through the project I became nervous. There was so much one could say about Huxley. How could I condense such a rich life and body of work into a 30-minute class? It had been a long time since my eighth grade speech. Could I still be effective in front of a group? Would I stumble and sound ridiculous? Would my fellow classmates be interested in the topic?

The day came to teach my class. I was well prepared but scared by so many unknowns. When it was my turn to teach, I took a deep breath, stood in front of the room, and guided my classmates into the brave new world of Aldous Huxley. At one point during the class, like my dodge ball game in high school, I entered the zone. Stories about Huxley, insights into his philosophy and books and the personal meaning his work had for me flowed seamlessly. My classmates were engaged. They were interested, asked questions and offered opinions. Thirty minutes passed like thirty seconds. I had achieved another breakthrough that would stay with me.

To be or not to be

There was a time, however, when I wasn't sure that communication skills stayed with you. It seemed they could one day fade away. Toward the end of his life my father lived in the Actor's Fund retirement home in New Jersey. I visited him often, but increasingly the visits became short. The avid communicator, entrancing storyteller and accomplished actor were no longer in evidence. He mostly looked down at the floor, said a few words and in a while it was time for me to go.

One night I said goodbye and walked through the dark empty halls of the retirement home, attempting to find my wife who was earlier speaking with one of the residents. Wandering about, basically lost, I eventually ran into someone and asked for directions to the exit and to the section where my wife was located. The young lady asked my name. As soon as I said it, her eyes lit up. She asked if I was Coby's son. I said yes, to which she replied, "I am Beth, the social worker here, and I have been trying to contact you for some time. Your father forgot your phone number and address, so I didn't have a way to reach you. I want to tell you something."

Several weeks prior, a director and cameraman had come to the retirement home to film a short documentary about the lives of the residents. At the heart of the film was the idea we shouldn't forget that dwelling within these walls were people who had lived rich lives. They were once dancers, poets, directors, writers and actors. Their skills, their artistry, were still alive within them. As Beth filled me in on all of this, I wondered what it had to do with my father. That's when she offered what she had been waiting to tell me. "In the film, your father appears and recites some lines from Shakespeare. Why don't we find your wife and we can watch the film together."

I thought she had made a mistake. My father hardly talks anymore. His greatest excitement, as I learned from the head of the retirement home, appears to be breaking the house rules by sneaking cigarettes into his room. Reciting Shakespeare? I don't think so. Oh yes, she countered. Let's go see.

A few minutes later I sat with my wife on a couch in Beth's office. She turned a TV on, put a video cassette into the player and the movie began. Midway through, there was my father lying in bed, looking directly at the camera, contemplating the eternal question: "To be or not to be . . ." He recited part of Hamlet's soliloquy flawlessly. All of the communication and acting skills were still with him; the enunciation, the pauses, the conviction, the emotion, the artistry, the total believability. It seemed like a miracle unfolding frame by precious frame. Beth turned to me with a look that seemed to say, "Isn't it amazing. The artistry is still alive, despite what you might have thought." She had a beaming smile on her face; as did I.

Paying tribute

I didn't know then that my father would pass away in a few months. I also didn't know that years later I would tell the story of that night. Having entered a Toastmasters regional public-speaking contest, I needed to write a speech. I decided it was time to share how my father and many others had inspired me; how they taught me that communicating as well as you can is its own reward and that the breakthroughs you make stay with you.

I was apprehensive about the speech. Would I be overcome with emotion? Could I communicate my message in a way that did justice to those who had encouraged me? Did I have the capability to effectively deliver a few lines of Shakespeare?

Sitting in my chair, waiting, I felt my concerns dissolve. This was not about me. It was about my father and countless mentors who helped me believe in the power of the written and spoken word. They showed me that communication counts, perhaps more than anything. This was their story. When it was my turn to speak, I took a deep breath, stood in front of my audience, and paid tribute to them.

References

Allgeier, S. (2009) *The Personal Credibility Factor*. Upper Saddle River, NJ: FT Press.

Bedell, G. (2000) *3 Steps to Yes*. New York: Three Rivers Press.

Bennis, W. and Nanus, B. (1985) *Leaders: Strategies for Taking Charge*. New York: Harper Collins.

Buffett, W. (2004–2005) *Berkshire Hathaway Annual Reports, 2004–2005*. Omaha, NE: Berkshire Hathaway.

Chernow, R. (1998) *Titan: The Life of John D. Rockefeller, Sr*. New York: Random House.

Covey, S.R. (1989) *The 7 Habits of Highly Effective People*. New York: Fireside, Simon & Schuster, 1989.

Covey, S.M.R. (2006) *The Speed of Trust*. New York: Free Press.

Demitropoulos, B. (2010) "Good communication good business," *American Business Magazine*. Retrieved 5 April 2013 from *www.americanbusinessmag.com/2010/04/good-communication-good-business*

Ericsson, K.A., Prietula, M.J., and Cokely, E.T. (2007) "The making of an expert." *Harvard Business Review*, July/August. Retrieved 11 October 2013 from *http://www.uvm.edu/~pdodds/files/papers/others/everything/ericsson2007a.pdf*

Fugere, B., Hardaway, C. and Warshawsky, J. (2005) *Why Business People Speak like Idiots*. New York: Free Press.

Goodwin, D.K. (2005) *Team of Rivals: The Political Genius of Abraham Lincoln*. New York: Simon & Schuster.

Hendricks, K. and Hendricks, G. (2004) *Attracting Genuine Love*. Boulder, CO: Sounds True.

Hutchens, A.K. (2002) *Brain Brilliant*. Atlanta, GA: AmyK International Publishing.

Jackson, T. (1998) *Inside Intel: Andy Grove and the Rise of the World's Most Powerful Chip Company*. New York: Plume.

Jones, D. (2006) "CEOs vouch for the waiter rule: watch how people treat staff." *USA Today*, 14 April 2006.

Leeds, D. (2000) *The 7 Powers of Questions: Secrets to Successful Communication in Life and at Work*. New York: Perigee Trade.

Levine, R.V. (2003) *The Power of Persuasion: How We're Bought and Sold*. Hoboken, NJ: John Wiley & Sons.

Lutz, W. (1996) *The New Doublespeak*. New York: HarperCollins.

Malone, C. (2011) "Can you hear me now? Web-enabled brand experiences that cut through the clutter." *Forbes* magazine. Retrieved 20 April 2013 from *http://*

www.forbes.com/sites/onmarketing/2011/11/03/can-you-hear-me-now-web-enabled-brand-experiences-that-cut-through-the-clutter/

Mandela, N. (1994) *Long Walk to Freedom*. Boston: Little, Brown & Company.

Manes, S. and Andrews, P. (1983) *Gates*. New York, Doubleday.

Orwell, G. (2002) *Essays*. New York: Everyman's Library.

Osteen, J. (2004) *Your Best Life Now*. New York: Time Warner Book Group.

Parker-Pope, T. (2011) "Six-Word Memoirs: the contest winners," *New York Times*. Retrieved 12 April 2013 from *http://well.blogs.nytimes.com/2011/05/17/six-word-momoirs-the-%20contest-winners/*

Payne, S.L. (1980) *The Art of Asking Questions*. Princeton, NJ: Princeton University Press, 1980.

Randall, C.B. (1964) *Making Good in Management: Reflections on the Challenges and Opportunities of a Business Career*. New York: McGraw Hill.

Rankin, H.J. (1999) *Power Talk: The Art of Effective Communication*. Hilton Head Island, SC: Step Wise Press.

Schell, G.R. (1999) *Bargaining for Advantage: Negotiation Strategies for Reasonable People*. New York: Viking.

Sellers, P. (2012) "The rehabilitation of Brenda Barnes," *FORTUNE* magazine. Retrieved 12 September 2013 from *http://postcards.blogs.fortune.cnn.com/2012/09/24/mpw-brenda-barnes/*

Shell, G.R. and Moussa, M. (2008) *The Art of Woo: Using Strategic Persuasion to Sell Your Ideas*. New York: Penguin Books.

Simmons, A. (2006) *The Story Factor*. New York: Basic Books.

Sloan, A. Jr. (1963) *My Years with General Motors*. New York: Doubleday.

Trump, D. (1987) *The Art of the Deal*. New York, Random House.

USDL (2011) *The American Time User Survey*. Washington, D.C.: Bureau of Labor Statistics, United States Department of Labor. Retrieved 17 April 2013 from *http://www.bls.gov/tus/charts/*

Waitley, D. (1995) *Empires of the Mind*. New York: William Morrow.

Watson, J. (2007) *Business Writing Basics*. North Vancouver, BC, Canada: Self-Counsel Press.

Wright, B. (2013) "Time to 'demise' ridiculous banking double-speak," *Financial News*. Retrieved 7 May 2013 from *www.efinancialnews.com/story/2013-23/hsbc-job-cuts-statement-english-language*

Zinsser, W. (2006) *On Writing Well*. New York: HarperCollins.

Index

Printed and bound by CPI Group (UK) Ltd, Croydon, CR0 4YY

08/05/2025

01864975-0001